YOU CAN ENJOY LIFE—
ON YOUR *OWN* TERMS!

Your dreams *can* come true! Whatever they are—breaking out of a rut, changing careers, developing hidden talents you've put on hold—you *do* have an option on a new and better life.

You'll discover why you fear making a change, how to confront it, and how to stick with your new commitment. You'll learn where destructive sources of guilt originate, and how to get rid of them. You'll understand why talking to others about making a move is a big mistake, while relying on your own judgment is the *only sure way*.

First, you must believe in yourself. Then, you can change your life. You want your chance, don't you? *FEEL FREE* can help you to start *now*—to make your plans, follow through, and get whatever you *really* want!

DAVID VISCOTT, M.D., is the bestselling author of: *The Making of a Psychiatrist, The Language of Feelings, How to Live with Another Person, Risking, Taking Care of Business, Winning* and *The Viscott Method* (ALL AVAILABLE FROM POCKET BOOKS). He hosts one of America's most popular syndicated radio talk shows, enjoyed by millions of listeners across the country. Dr. Viscott lives in Los Angeles, California.

Books by David S. Viscott, M.D.

Feel Free
How to Live with Another Person
The Language of Feelings
The Making of a Psychiatrist
Risking
Taking Care of Business
The Viscott Method: A Revolutionary Program
  for Self-Analysis and Self-Understanding
Winning

Published by POCKET BOOKS

Most Pocket Books are available at special quantity discounts for bulk purchases for sales promotions, premiums or fund raising. Special books or book excerpts can also be created to fit specific needs.

For details write the office of the Vice President of Special Markets, Pocket Books, 1230 Avenue of the Americas, New York, New York 10020.

Feel Free

David Viscott, M.D.

PUBLISHED BY POCKET BOOKS NEW YORK

Names, locations and all other identifying details of case histories have been carefully altered throughout this book to ensure fully the privacy of all concerned.

Originally published by Peter H. Wyden, Inc.

TO MY PARENTS

For of all sad words of tongue or pen,
The saddest are these: "It might have been."

John Greenleaf Whittier
from *Maud Muller*

CONTENTS

*Feel
Free*

1

RUN FOR
YOUR LIFE

The chances are, if you're really honest with yourself, that you won't do it this year either. You'll stay in the same situation, in the same role, in spite of how much you hate it. You'll probably stay married to the same person, no matter how many reasons you can give for leaving. You'll put off doing all of the things you claim you really want to do, in spite of how much you say you want to do them. The only new situation you're likely to experience one year from now is that you'll be one year older and, unless that is the fulfillment of some secret dream, you'll still be making plans for the year after this, plans that will have as much of a chance of coming true as this year's.

Admit it, for once face the fact that you often feel like running. That's the word, running. Packing up your bags, putting on your hat and coat, taking some money out of the bank, filling the car up with gas and just going. Maybe, if you have a flair for the dramatic, you'd even take time to write a note: "I'm tired of living my life just to make everyone else happy. I'm finally going to do what *I* want."

And who could blame you? Look around. All over the country people are finding themselves. Kids are leaving home, dropping out of school, saying "no" to the rat race, trying to find a simpler life that they can relate to. Trying to find values that they can really believe in. Okay, so they're lost. A lot of them *are* lost! Okay, so it's something that they'll grow out of. You've probably said that yourself a dozen times. You probably believe it. It might even be true. They might grow out of it and settle down.

Believe it, if it makes you feel better. But what about *you?* Why is it that you haven't grown out of it? Why is it that much of the time you aren't really doing what you want, aren't really happy where you are or whom you are with? What's holding *you* back?

Look at this new culture that's emerging all around. Sexual standards are drastically changing, it seems. Kids don't feel as guilty as you did about getting involved with others. Their attitudes do seem healthier, more natural, even though it's hard to admit it when it happens to be your daughter. Anyway, the kids don't seem to be worrying about morals for morals' sake. They casually accept and partake in many of the things you have secretly yearned for. You probably feel left out, as if you were born too late, as if life has passed you by. And sex is only one small part of it. Admit it, you feel jealous. That's right, of your own kids, jealous.

Let's look at how this applies to women as well as men. Ladies first.

Many women are feeling the growing tremors of the Women's Liberation Movement. It looks tempting to protest, to give up the role you've been playing. You've probably been secretly protesting for years anyhow.

How many meals prepared on time, sat down to late (and eaten with arguments and fighting) will it take for you to realize that you can't expect complete fulfillment by being a housewife? This idea really isn't new to you. You've seen television commercials where a self-assured older model says, "I'm a housewife and I love it," and thought to yourself, "She's got to be crazy."

Who in your home really notices what you do? Not just claims to notice what you do, but really appreciates all the little things you do? It would take a list as long as both of your arms to put down the things you do in a day that others don't even notice or take for granted. Many books have been written to rationalize housekeeping, to make you believe that it can be an art, a challenge, a totally engrossing way to spend your life. But you don't really believe it.

Perhaps it's true that if you didn't do the housework, no one else would. But it's also true that you invent much of the work you do. Inventing work is a way of life that you were taught. Congratulations! You have inherited the world's most complex system for keeping busy. Busy? Why? Just what is it that you would do if you weren't so busy? What really hurts is that you've also been taught to expect others to appreciate you for being busy, for doing what you really don't like. You may even have learned how to use being unappreciated—to use it as a weapon.

Do you really want to live like this? Would you want to spend your life with a husband who walks around the house checking how shiny your floors are, how clean your wash is and how white your whites are? Who really deep down believes that your busy-work is terribly important? It would be like living with a zealot-drudge.

The pressures under which you live and survive as a housewife are like being pinned down by enemy gunfire while loudspeakers are playing records from home. The world of television commercials—drawing its situations and people from a world where no one can really exist—has probably convinced some part of you that you're a failure, at least by comparison to that special world on the screen. Even if you are aware of the absurdity of the TV situations (which you watch even if you ridicule them), the fact that you do watch them begins to erode your sense of contentment. Television has gotten to you, even if it only appears to make you laugh. And why shouldn't it get to you? You're television's main target.

The television composite of the ideal woman reveals a slender, attractive, well-coiffed, well-dressed woman, eternally twenty-seven, twenty-nine at the most. You are supposed to be like her. At least you are supposed to want to be like her. No matter what kind of mess the children or the dog make, you are supposed to put on a mock angry look that soon gives way to a loving smile while you clean up. The culprit who has made the mess watches you and tells you what a good job of cleaning you've done. You give him a cookie as his reward.

You spend the rest of your afternoon removing stains from your children's clothes and compare your results with those of the neighbors. Then you proceed to clean your oven, which is hard work no matter what chemical miracles you use. Afterwards you settle back and examine your dishes for spots before the neighbors arrive for coffee.

When your husband comes home, he tells you he has a headache. You prescribe aspirin for him. He tells you that you look great. You tell him that's because you take care of yourself with vitamin supplements. He tells you you smell great. You tell him that's because you spray every part of your body that your various sprays can reach. He tells you you're not sweaty either. You just smile.

You are part chauffeur, part lover, part nurse, part accountant, part cook, part maid, part mother and, last and not least, part drudge. Are you appreciated? Just listen to what the critics say! When you scratch the car, you're told it's because you don't concentrate on your driving enough. If you're not passionate enough, you're told it's because you don't care, that you don't appreciate sex enough any more and won't rest and give yourself time to get in the mood. When you tell someone to get his own aspirin (it's right there in front of him and you feel you're coming down with the same ailment) you're told you're not compassionate. If you make a mistake in the checkbook, you've got a bad business head. Your cooking isn't what it used to be, you're missing cobwebs in the corners lately and you scream at the kids a lot. What's happening to you?

Look at that lady on the television screen asking you to guess how old she is. She looks better than you do, much better. Something's wrong somewhere. You have a problem. You don't believe that being a housewife is as great as it is supposed to be and yet you think that being a liberated woman is a little farfetched, maybe just as trumped up in its own way.

If you picked up and left today, you know everyone

would miss you. But would they miss the part of you that is the real you, the special one-of-a-kind you? Or would they just miss the part of you that they could replace by hiring someone else? Would they just miss the part that is special to them because of their relationship to you, the part that fulfills their needs? What about the part that is the fulfillment of your own needs, the part that is who you are? Perhaps that part has never, even yet, seen the light of day.

The busy-work that you have allowed to fill up your life is in the way, keeping you from doing what you may really want, not even allowing you to see that you want it. Much of the appreciation you now get is for things that you yourself really don't think much of. Even if you could approach the television standards, you wouldn't be happier, just cleaner. Is the answer another man, another life, a career, a part-time job somewhere? It's hard to think about. It's been such a long time since you've done anything on your own.

People who do real work are no better off, it seems. Look at that work week! Do you spend hours commuting, being uncomfortable, wrapped in choking smog and noisy traffic? And even more time at a tedious, thankless job that someone would try to give to a computer the moment they figure out how to program one to make your decisions?

You struggle to make ends meet and always feel at loose ends. You take vacations that you can't seem to enjoy and are afraid to be one day late getting back to work. The people who work around you seem distant, forced, perhaps anxious. After all, they don't like their job any more than you like yours. You're worried about getting ahead, so you jump headlong into more and more work, maybe just to try to keep from thinking about the problems at home or in your head or at work.

You feel unchallenged and unfulfilled much of the time. Instead of feeling content you feel frustrated and perhaps threatened. It often takes you hours to relax when you do get home and then you watch television just to keep from snapping at the family. Why are you doing all this? For a family that you secretly feel doesn't really appreciate you? For a household of material possessions that you either don't have time to enjoy—or resent because they are put away for special occasions and you don't rate being considered special in your own house? For your kids who seem unimpressed with what you give them? Only some kind of fool would knuckle under to working conditions like that.

What is going on? Without doubt, the youth of the past few decades is really different from the way you used to be and that difference is not because of the usual generation gap. Anyone who doesn't believe this, really hasn't looked. These kids have more freedom to be themselves than any other kids in history. Yet they seem too serious in a way, sometimes humorless, and their troubles seem different. They seem more concerned with relevance, with feelings and with sharing than they are with the acquisition of material things. Perhaps a good stiff dose of life will make them see things differently. Wait till they've gone out and tried to find a job or when they have the responsibilities of a home and kids. They'll change, maybe.

Maybe they won't. It just might be that they have given up trying to get things and be things because these are supposed to be the things to get and to be. It's hard to look at these kids without getting angry when you've struggled

7

to do your best, to provide what you think you should have gotten for them. Such as: a good home that they seldom come home to; good food on the table that they ignore; good clothes when they wear dungarees and surplus army jackets and don't even comb their hair; and a good education in a good school where they spend their time boycotting classes.

Doesn't anyone care about anything any more except you?

What would happen if you stopped caring quite so hard? Someone's got to care! Someone's got to do what he believes in, what he knows and has been taught is right. There's a job to do and it's got to be done. There's always a job to do. It seems kids don't understand that any more.

It was probably the atomic bomb. Maybe President Truman was right by dropping it and the war was cut short by thousands of casualties. Maybe he was wrong and all the pain and turmoil that resulted is still destroying the world. A lot more people died in that mushroom cloud that summer morning over Japan than lived in Hiroshima. The blinding flash that extinguished 100,000 lives destroyed a part of all children everywhere who were to follow. A generation of children grew up with the horrifying insight that their lives might also end in a flash of light—just like that. They knew that it was possible, any time at all, for a warhead, launched by some hidden and unknown force, to enter the atmosphere and to become a brilliant light that would end their life, that afterwards there might not even be anyone left to remember the fact that they once were.

So, you say, there's nothing new in that. You sat in the

living room listening to the radio reports of the bombings of Japan. Worse than that: you remember. You were moved, too. So what? It's not new and it explains nothing. What is the point of this digression? The point is: no generation growing up before ever knew so surely that death, the sudden and the unknown, could really happen. No other group of children ever had to deal with the prospect of their own death so early in life and so perfunctorily. Even in the worst times of war, the enemy used to have a name and a face. He was never a nameless force that kills everything, without discrimination, all the world, them. The concept of death is something that children in their early years are poorly equipped to deal with. Severe childhood losses often make an adult hypersensitive to later losses. Usually death is realistically dealt with for the first time around the age of nineteen, when youths grow into adults. At that time they mourn the death of their own childhood and learn to accept new roles.

What happened to the children who grew up knowing prematurely that they were one day, any day perhaps, likely to be killed? Death is the only priority that cannot be displaced; in the end it is the only sure winner. For the children born at the time of the bomb, death became an imminent possibility, even if they denied it (to believe in death is to stop being a child).

Many people who face death and later survive find that the experience has sharpened their perspective and reshaped their goals. It allows them to see themselves as they really are and wish to be and permits them to give up false ideas and to move on (which is why people believe that dying men tell the truth). Death became a reality for a generation of our children. It made them decide that life should be an endless possibility—and worth living. They decided that the rules are, after all, only rules and that everyone must find his own way and do what his spirit dictates. There may be no more time left, they feel. The future is now.

But what about you? You've known that you were going to die for some time now, but somehow that doesn't allow you to give up responsibilities or to run away and do what you secretly wish but have put off. The difference is that you have learned to deal with death as a distant event, as something that is acceptable, arriving at its own appropriate time. It is not so much the intrusive stranger as it is a friend whose arrival is expected in the end of one's years, taking away the pain when drugs have failed, when the eyes are dim and the dreamer dreams no more.

Although you believe that you will die, you do not believe that you are *about* to die. You postpone your dreams, content that something will happen to change things some day. You tell yourself that life isn't really all *that* bad, that you have much of what you want in spite of how you sometimes feel, in spite of whatever you've said or how bleakly these few pages have made life appear.

Maybe there is only one way for you to understand. Imagine for a moment that you are about to board an aircraft returning home. You become ill and miss your flight. After a while, you feel better and sit in the waiting room deciding which flight to take. It is announced that the flight you just missed has crashed into the sea. You sink back in shock, realizing you have narrowly missed being killed. You remember that your name was on the flight list and decide to call home and tell everyone, but you stop for a moment and think.

As far as the world knows, you are dead. Your responsibilities have ended. Your wife is about to receive some large insurance payments and will be able to manage very well, a tribute to your foresight and responsibility, not to mention a very pushy insurance salesman. That competitive colleague at your office, the one who has been pressuring you, can now take over your job. It may be rough on your family, but not for long. People do get over this sort of thing. After a respectable period of time, your wife will probably remarry. You probably even know the fellow. Good luck to them. As a matter of fact, good luck to you. Here you are, alive and well, presumed dead by all, with a pocketful of uncashed travelers checks which, if you move fast enough, you can redeem without anyone being the wiser. The company will never know. You will have enough to live on for months, until you decide what you really want to do.

Go ahead, take the next taxi into town. Better make that a bus because you are going to need the money to keep going until you get settled. You need time to think things over, to decide what you want to do now, now that you have no responsibilities. Except to stay alive.

You don't want to do anything? You don't *have* to do anything. That's right, and who is going to know? No one is going to come up to you and ask you why you're not doing something constructive. Why should they care? For the most part, people seemed to care about whatever you used to do because you *thought* they cared, because you made it seem important.

I can understand your feelings about wanting to know how everyone is taking your demise. That's only natural. Look at that funeral service. No casket in sight anywhere.

And flowers! Didn't you specifically say, no flowers? Look at the faces in the front row. Look at all those tears. One would think, what with all that display of emotion, they would have shown some of it when you were around—or maybe just listened to you when you said something. Too many things got in the way then, I suppose. Too many little battles obscuring what was real. Why are all your wife's friends, even the ones you can't stand, crying harder than she is? Especially the one with the red scarf!

The kids do look sad, genuinely sad. Or are they just shocked? I suppose it's all right for you to feel a little guilty, running out on them like this. One of their friends you can't stand is saying something reassuring. You know he doesn't mean it. There are all your relatives. This doesn't make sense. You know your brother-in-law doesn't feel that sad, not after your last phone conversation and the names he called you. Thank goodness you're not your sister and don't have to live with him. You don't have to live with anyone you don't want to, not now, not any more. The feelings that everyone is showing at the funeral are so different from what they expressed to you when you were alive. Do their feelings about you now have more to do with themselves than with you? Maybe people in the end are really unable to think much about others. Perhaps people care only when they themselves are involved. Maybe your brother-in-law is upset only because he feels guilty because he called you names.

It's a large crowd, though. Maybe it's this big because everyone knew there was no body and they wouldn't have to go to the cemetery. There are your old golf partners. What a shame to break up a foursome that's been together so long. I wonder who they'll play with now? Will they play this Sunday? Wouldn't you? Who do you think they'll get? They'll find someone. You can always get a fourth. You used to say that all the time.

Everyone is settling down for the eulogy. Who is that walking up to the lectern? You don't know him. What about the guy you've known all your life? Where the hell is he? Someone remarks that it's a shame your old friend is out of town and that a stranger will have to give the eulogy on short notice, based on what he learned from the family about you. Just *your* luck.

"He was a fine man. He was a good man. He was a man who loved his family, a man who loved his children. He loved them more, in fact, than anything else in this world. He was not a complicated man, but a straightforward man, an honest man, who said what he believed and believed in what he did."

Where did they get this guy from?

"He struggled to give his family the opportunities which he himself never had, to give them the chances which fortune had not favored him with. But he did not curse his task or complain or even doubt for a moment in the worth of what he did."

It's no use yelling. He can't hear you.

"He looked always to the future, treated people as he found them and gave of himself that special part when others asked, and he gave it without reservation."

Why is everyone crying and nodding agreement? Even you don't understand what this guy is saying.

"He was not a religious man in the strict sense of the word. I mean, he was not pious. He was, rather, religious in the true sense of the word; that is, in the deed, in the doing. He gave to his children a home and love and to his wife companionship and understanding.''

Maybe he is making this up as he goes on.

"His life was an example of hard work and self-sacrifice which we can all profit from. Let the lesson of his being, his ardor and simplicity be heard by all of us. He did not seek to single himself out to find personal glory. He did not strive to live some carefree, meaningless existence where pleasure for pleasure's sake was the principle which governed his life. He knew his duty. He understood his obligations. He gathered his forces and lived. He has reminded us once again of how little one need do in life, how narrowly one can live and still feel the broad pulse of the human experience, yes, still live a life that one can truly call worthwhile.''

I admit he missed the best things you did, the hole-in-one on the third at Pinecrest, that fantastic first girl when you were eighteen, but he also missed the worst—like blowing up one of *our* tanks in the war, remember? But he didn't know you. He was a stranger. Yes, you can understand that, but why are all the people whom you did know agreeing with him? Are you a stranger to them, too? Why was there no mention of some of your plans, the things you've wanted to do for years? What was all this about self-sacrifice, as if that had been a matter of personal choice?

You wanted to do other things. You had a lot of ideas, projects to do once the mortgage was paid off, the kids were through school and you had taken care of everyone else. Maybe your own business, doing something with your hands, a little farm, your own little inn somewhere. Maybe just taking a job you liked more. You'd be able to afford it then. They really weren't such crazy ideas. Why didn't he mention those ideas? Even if he didn't know you, your family did. Maybe they never listened. Maybe they thought you weren't serious or that your ideas weren't that important, just crazy ideas.

It's over already? They're all leaving. Wait! Nobody knows what you were really like! No one took the time to tell them. But maybe you can't tell people what you would really like to do. Maybe you have to do it or else no one takes you seriously. No one ever takes you seriously.

Look, you can't spend the day dreaming about this funeral. You've got to run and catch that bus and get into town. Are you in luck for missing that plane! Run for that bus. You still have time to do what you want. Get on it. Run! Don't even look back—no one at the funeral did. Run for your life.

Why does it have to be this way? Why can't you look at your life now and alter it the way you really want to, take some risks and discover life again? Most people are trapped in a secret world of unfulfilled wishes, suffering unspeakable aches when their silent expectations—the dreams of what they would like in life—do not materialize. They mourn not being allowed to do things that, deep inside, they know they could do if only they got the chance or just took the time to try. Everyone feels this way to some degree. Somehow life manages to become very busy and fills up all of our time and all of our lives with tasks that seem very important for us to do but leave us with little personal satisfaction or even sense of pride or even a feeling of our own individuality in the end.

If, when it's all done, we remain anonymous to those who attend our funeral, it is because we were content to remain unknown to ourselves. Why should legions of people feel desperate and discouraged in the face of abundance and opportunity? The many reasons lie as much within us as without.

This book is a guide, an attempt to look at the forces that hold people back from fulfilling their dreams. It is meant for people who have already gotten someplace, but are not sure they like where they are. It looks at the fears, the pressures, the obligations, the self-defeats and the self-made prisons that keep people from finding fulfillment, love, self-expression and happiness. There is a way to enjoy life on your own terms. Nothing is for nothing and all changes have their cost. Becoming free, taking charge of what your life is, is not easy and not always pleasurable. It is asking you to accept your own happiness as a goal and to be responsible for attaining it. Being free and not being free are not comparable conditions. Being free is a totality unto itself, both feared and wanted more than anything else. Without it, life has no flavor and darkness no promise of hope.

Even if conditions at home and at work seem in control, life may still be unsatisfying and lonely. The obstacles that get between us and the other selves we know to exist inside are the fear of changing, the fear of self-confrontation and the fear that we may not be good enough to go our own way, forsaking custom and the unsmiling crowd. How good does a wish have to be before it can be fulfilled, how important an idea before it can be followed, how rich a talent before it can be developed?

We find ourselves trapped, too many of us, between conflicting standards. On one side we are cajoled into performing busy-work and into accepting it as a reasonable goal, worthy of all our attention. On the other side, we observe people with exaggerated abilities against whom we dare not compete. Between the ridiculous made to appear sublimely fulfilling, and the sublime made to appear ridiculously aloof, we spend our lives trying to find our way out.

The way is us.

In one person's life, his ability is all he has. If he believes in it and tries to break away and finds himself, he feels complete and in charge of his own destiny.

Come on, you feel it. Allow yourself to have whatever you really want. Isn't it time at last that you have your chance?

2

DO LESS, GET MORE

If you've left a roast burning in the oven or a client calling frantically to find out where in the world you are and you are reading this while waiting for your flight to Tahiti to be announced in the airport lounge, you have decided to run all right, but you've probably not decided much else. Not yet, anyway. You've got a lot of work ahead of you, and not just figuring out what to do in Tahiti after your savings run out. A good place to start is to find out why you never decided to run before.

For one thing, you became confused, anxious or overwhelmed by a lot of conflicting facts. Such as the fact that you've got a lot to lose. If you do make a major change in your life, involving the way you see the world and the way you live, you will have to give up much that you now consider important.

You may discover that only through giving up some of the material things that you are now afraid of losing will it be possible to become free; your possessions have restricted you and kept you trapped where you are. You may find that your home, your furnishings, the social engagements you claim you can not do without—all have taken so much of your energy and time to maintain that you are really not free to do anything you wish.

Come on, take a look at the choices that are available to you. Don't be afraid. The worst that can happen is that you'll find out that you want more out of life. Is that so bad? I promise to be as gentle as possible. I don't want to frighten you or make you feel miserable. All I want to do is to let you know that there are other possibilities for you in your life and to give you some idea why you haven't been able to get what you want. I want to show you exactly what keeps people from doing what they want to do.

The very first step in making any change is to become aware of the barriers that hold people back, especially the confusion of guilts, self-imposed financial burdens and traditions that keep people in their places.

You are the only person who controls your destiny in this world, no matter how much you may think otherwise. In order to allow you to take charge, you have to know what has kept you back. You may not like everything you see when you take a real look at yourself, but if you can then do what you want, the effort is worthwhile.

You can do anything that pleases you. Maybe the time has come to change that career of yours, if you haven't been moving along the way you want. Perhaps one should always have more than one career in life. A person who is alive changes and grows. The choices one makes for oneself at one time in life are likely to be less meaningful later on. People's needs change. Once you may have wanted security in the form of regular hours and pay; now you may find it stifling. Where being a homemaker might have once offered fulfillment and challenge, you might now find it old and dull.

Though it is probably not true for most people, some spouses grow so apart from each other in outlook and feeling that if they met now they might not even be friends, let alone husband and wife.

The notion implied by the marriage contract—that two people have the capacity to satisfy all of the needs of the other for a lifetime—would be amusing if it were not so widely supported by the establishment. It just isn't possible. Indeed, how on earth could it be? Two people who marry in their twenties ideally grow up. From the person they once were they become someone else. As the years go by, they are bound to discover more about themselves and require outlets besides those that the spouse can provide. The great majority of these new needs have nothing to do with sex; they have to do with being understood; with attitudes about life, feelings, and people. If a spouse doesn't fulfill all the other's needs this does not mean a divorce is indicated. It only means that each spouse must find some fulfillment on his own terms. Not to do so is to expect a spouse to solve all one's needs. And this is not possible because human beings aren't built that way.

The worst that can happen in anyone's marriage is to hate one's spouse for not being what one wants and not being able to appreciate him for what he is. In many troubled marriages partners blame each other only to find their relationship greatly improved once each begins to do what he wants in life and stops hating the other for holding him back.

Maybe it's time to buy a small farm and raise cattle. Maybe you want to move to the southern coast of Spain and spend your days fishing or making films. Perhaps you want that small inn in the country so you can act as cook and waiter, bartender and story teller. Perhaps you would just like to take life easier and stop running so hard after a paycheck every week.

Some women may protest that it is too difficult to begin a new life with a bunch of kids screaming and messing up the place and with meals to make. With young children it *is* difficult, but as they become independent it's possible to do more. But it's first necessary to eliminate activities from your life that do nothing whatever for you—except consume time. The social interchanges with other women at the market are neither very social nor very helpful for your marketing. You can't really discuss problems at length or even gossip in privacy and you can't concentrate on shopping. If you plan, you can eliminate much wasted time.

As for those car pools and being an errand boy, you might just learn to say "No." Contrary to what you may believe, the world will not fall apart. Since children do not really know what they are eating, you can make and freeze weeks of sandwiches at once. I can see eyebrows being raised. But your kids probably won't know any better and, what's worse, don't appreciate it when you do more. When they don't appreciate you, you feel badly. Do yourself a favor, do less. That's the beauty of the "Feel Free" approach: you'll get more out of your effort by putting less in. It's like repealing income taxes. The kids will love your unfrozen tuna fish sandwiches and you'll be a hero for having an inexhaustible supply ever ready.

Why not travel? Look, there's a whole world out there that you've been promising yourself you'd run to when you got the chance: Mexico, Europe, the Far East. Here's your chance! You can do it as well now as almost any other time. It's still not too late. You don't have to spend your life sighing through travel magazines. There's a less complicated life for you somewhere, a life where you can be happy and enjoy being you every day. There's no need to stay miserable about conditions that you can change: nasty bosses, crabby neighbors, and being trapped in a spiral of demands to earn more, spend more, borrow more.

You probably can get what you want with what you've already got. You can grow flowers, paint, sing, weave, build, love, loaf, or just take time to dream. Perhaps all you really want is time to think things over. The deep down trouble with all these attractive plans (or anything like them) is that they are opposite to what "nice" people are supposed to do with the best years of their lives. You're supposed to wait till you retire and are too old to enjoy them.

Why wait?

Lately a large number of reports have been appearing about people who have decided to quit and find new lives for themselves. In 1968, *Time* magazine published an essay expanding on F. Scott Fitzgerald's comment that "There are no second acts in American lives." It indicated how many difficulties Americans make for themselves by staying in the same role.

Since then many other articles have appeared. In June 1970, *Life* described five people who decided to change their careers and switch to more satisfying ones. One man left a sales career to become a captain in the National Guard Eskimo Scouts. Another gave up being a stockbroker to study ecology. A third gave up being an insurance broker to operate a small inn. A veterinarian became a laborer because he was fed up with the pressures. A policeman became an artist.

The *Wall Street Journal*, of all establishment media, repeatedly described executives who left the safe life. In February 1971, two front page stories dealt invitingly with numerous successful men quitting the corporate world. In March, the Long Island newspaper *Newsday* celebrated a policeman and his family who decided to follow one of their dreams; they gave up the security of home and job to go West to open up a campground. The same month, *Los Angeles Magazine* reported on "The New Dropouts." It mentioned an executive who became an innkeeper, a publisher who decided to write, and a construction worker who was all set to circumnavigate the globe.

As if by collusion, *The National Observer* and *The New York Times* both came out with articles on the middle age syndrome on April 5, 1971. Both stressed the desperateness, the depression and the sense of being trapped that many people come to feel in the middle of their lives when they sense that what they have been doing doesn't suit them. And a few days later *Newsday* pointed out some of the solutions to problems facing people who were trying to change careers within the academic world.

As if to capture the spirit of the entire growing movement, the *Boston Globe* carried a story in May about a physicist who left the world of exotic research to run away with the circus and become a clown.

Look at all of this happening right under your nose! And this is only a small part of what is going on. People *can* leave what they have been doing. They *can* begin new lives. They *can* find themselves. *You* can do it, too. There is no need to sit and feel trapped. Once you know the ropes you, too, can find your way out.

Now about those ropes. Our society, in many ways, is very rigid and restricting. Its traditional point of view is that one must be constructive and lead a productive life that is neatly planned and worked out. Young people are expected to set clear-cut goals and directions for themselves, often even before they finish high school, and to make decisions based on these ideas. For instance, they are supposed to decide what to do with all the rest of their lives.

Some people do know what they want to do when they are quite young. Most often this happens to the exceptionally talented who have already achieved some degree of fulfillment in some specialty. The rest of us usually choose a way of life with which we are only vaguely familiar. In fact, many people choose careers based on what they wish were true about themselves, not what they have discovered to be true. This is not an accident. It cannot be instantly corrected. It is a problem that can only be solved by allowing people more time to give up old ideas and discover who they are.

The notion that one must devote life to hard work or to bringing up a family as soon as one is out of school does not take into consideration that human beings by nature usually do not know what they really want when they are young or that change is part of the human condition. The fact that we do not change as much as we should while growing up is not proof that we do not want to change. It is evidence that society exerts very strong pressures upon us to conform from the very start.

People need a great deal of time to discover who they really are. All beginnings are only tentative; merely attempts. How can the strivings of young people be anything else? They do not know what they want because they do not yet know who they are. Young people often do what they *think* they should be doing. They may know what they feel in any given moment and still be unaware of who they are, unaware of what they would feel in another situation. Young people tend to react to each situation as it occurs. It is only when one is able to act based upon a broader sense of personal identity, and can predict how one would react in the future, that real goals can be chosen. This takes time, more time than society has thought fit or decent to allow.

"Back to work. You can't waste time like this," you've been told. Well, the time to reconsider your goals is now.

It's too bad that society demands major life commitments at a time when one is least able to understand what one is getting into. How many people decided on their college major because it was the only department without classes on Saturday or before ten in the morning? How many people took the major that looked easiest, or required no long thesis? We make our life decisions based on very flimsy motivations sometimes. Enjoying life and taking it easy—that's how it is when you're young. The difficulty comes when you have to apply your background and training to life, to earn a living by being the person you became because, once upon a time, it didn't seem important to be able to think hard before ten o'clock in the morning.

A person must have the opportunity to reject the choices that he has made in his youth, to renounce past mistakes. The idea that young people should be more mature and make better choices for themselves may have merit in terms of society, but it just isn't possible. Young people are young people. That means that they are going to keep on making mistakes in choosing what they want to become and in evaluating who they are. To eliminate some of the pain that results from these premature (and therefore bad) decisions, one must reverse them and start anew. This is true whether the original decision was made one year ago or two decades ago. It is never too late to find what is right for you. Somehow society has failed us by not allowing us a moment to breathe and change course.

3
WHAT'S BEEN KEEPING YOU?

Before most of us knew who we were or what was happening to us we found ourselves knee deep in commitments and more commitments. Sometimes the commitments were to goals we really wanted, like a new house or a more luxurious style of life. In time, unfortunately, we allow such commitments to grow out of proportion so that they require more and more time and energy to maintain them and give us less and less enjoyment and freedom.

This happens because we become committed to our roles very early in life, before we are sure of ourselves or had a chance to try out other careers and attitudes. Eventually the investments we made in our world became so great that even though the results were not always fulfilling we feared disrupting them and losing whatever we had worked for.

We are so concerned about maintaining the commitments of years ago, when we were largely ignorant of ourselves, that when we finally know who we are we feel too tied down to go after what we really want. No wonder that the way out is not always obvious.

Mike and Alice have been married fifteen years, since

their early twenties. Both are college graduates, both bright and industrious. Mike always wanted to be an architect. Because his father was in the construction business, he decided to get a degree in engineering, go on to graduate school and finally work with his father as a designer-builder. But father's business collapsed shortly before graduation. Mike put aside his plans to become an architect and started working for a big company as an engineer. He really didn't like the job or the profession. He only became an engineer as a step to something else, but the something else had disappeared—or so he thought. Alice had studied dance in college and was thought to show some promise. She had hoped that after marriage she would be able to begin a career as a dancer. But there never seemed to be enough time, so when she became pregnant, she, too, put aside her plans.

Mike began to do well, and as he brought more money home, Alice found new ways to use it. Upset because she did not have the opportunity to follow her career, she decided to make the life (which circumstances had forced her to accept) more pleasant. She began to surround herself with luxuries that made her feel less uncomfortable: better drapes, better rugs, better everything, a soft balm of material possessions. This occurred slowly and insidiously. Mike and Alice were only aware that there was less money left over for doing what they both loved. The more he earned, the less they seemed to have.

When Alice asks, "You want a nice home, don't you?" Mike nods "Yes." Mike and Alice *do* have a very nice home. Mike has plans to get out of the company and start a business of his own someday, maybe doing something with architecture after all. But that takes money and risk, and in the past few years he hasn't been able to save anything. There are always expenses that come first: the insurance, the children's education, medical bills, food bills, household bills. When Mike and Alice go over their budget to cut down, they always start with bare essentials and end up with the same list and in the same restrictive financial position.

How do you save enough to do what you want?

It is obvious that Mike and Alice are stuck. They can't reduce their expenditures, even with the help of a financial advisor, because that is simply not what the problem is. The problem is not financial. The financial problem is only a symptom of a kind of conspiracy of material acquisition.

Mike is not stupid. He's a good engineer. He can give a sharp cost analysis for any of the products he helped to develop. He is a rather witty conversationalist. Alice by no means is inactive. She reads all the latest books and talks intelligently about world affairs and the children's problems. In her fifteen years of marriage she has participated in several organizations and served as president in one of them. In spite of all this, neither partner feels complete.

What is the matter with this couple? Why do they feel trapped?

Alice, hurt because her career was ended, became withdrawn. Not withdrawn in the way we usually think of it, not avoiding friends, shutting the blinds, but withdrawn from her own special self. The world no longer appeared full of new ways to grow but became merely a place where she had to live. Her home became her retreat for herself. Which is why she filled her house with new possessions,

possessions that she and Mike had always said they wanted. Possessions that, surprisingly, seemed easier to get than they imagined. After all, if you want something material, you just buy it when you have enough money. It is much harder to make dreams come true. No store offers easy financing of dreams.

Mike was not happy with his position. Although he changed jobs several times over the years, he remained in engineering because he said that was where he could get the best money. He really wasn't skilled to do anything else. He could have retrained for another job, but that would have taken too long and the demand of the family's financial commitments made that unrealistic. It was too great a risk to retrain for a job in which Mike did not seem all that interested. So he stayed on and began to earn more money. And they went on spending more on the house, more on almost everything. Actually Mike took great pride in seeing the house enlarge and fill up and even greater pride when they moved to a larger house. The house became concrete proof that what he had done had worth to it. If ever he feared that sacrificing his career as an architect was a mistake, all he needed to do was to look at that house, those fixtures, that paneling in the den, to know that here was some measure of his worth, that his life was *not* a mistake.

This couple can't save because they use luxuries to placate their doubts about themselves. They are committed again and again, committed to spend. When expenses in one category go down, expenses in another go up. When a house symbolizes the security and worth of people who have compromised their dreams there will never be enough money saved to fulfill the original dreams.

There will never be enough left over to get what they really wanted. The objects that they substituted for their dreams eat up all of the funds, which makes the realization of dreams impossible.

Everything seems to work in reverse. Actually, if they could save, Alice and Mike have enough earning power to allow Alice to begin dancing again and for Mike to begin a new business. But with their present method of spending it is unlikely. Part of the reason is that in some way Alice and Mike began to acquire all their possessions to keep from confronting themselves. The longer Mike put off the idea of going into business for himself, the harder it became for him to think about it. He allowed Alice to buy what she did because it created new obligations which he in turn had to work harder to meet so he could tell himself that it was impossible for him to consider change. In fact, he may have encouraged her. Anyway, it now looked physically impossible for Mike to begin a new life. Even though he was afraid to try, he could not be blamed for working like a dog. It was so easy to fool himself and say that it wasn't his fault if he couldn't move on.

Alice played the same game, spending all her time keeping the house organized, balancing the strained budget and keeping their possessions in good condition. The plumbers, electricians, masons and all her other commitments required her constant attention. How could she have time even to think about what she really wanted to do? There was too much to do already. The house was serving its purpose. It crippled the minds of the people who lived in it so that they could only think of the symbol. They no longer knew what it symbolized. They only knew that they were not as happy as they thought they would be, but did not know why.

They have forgotten that they were once happier with less. The time they looked forward to, when they would have money to do what they wanted, passed unnoticed a long time ago, eclipsed by demands of possessions they really didn't need.

A strange thing begins to happen some time along the way. Each new acquisition seems less attractive. It is not quite perfect. It seems harder to find exactly what you want, because what you still want is to fulfill the old wish, not acquire new symbols that don't really make you feel better. It becomes more and more difficult to make the symbols work. You begin to travel to distant places to get the right fixtures for the lights or the right fabric for the sofa. A ritual develops that consumes more time as more money becomes available. Even when the cost of an object is a smaller percentage of the total income and it takes less work to acquire it, the physical difficulties—the shopping, waiting and matching that are now involved—keep up its special symbolic meaning. Acquiring possessions uses up time that might be spent doubting. The dreams of long ago can be kept still. You will never have enough time. There are things to be acquired.

More strangely, even though it may not always be noticeable at first, a faint note of resentment appears, expressing itself perhaps as disinterest or waning enthusiasm in acquiring. This has been felt before but was held in. Mike feels he really doesn't like the drapes or the new chair, even though he may have helped choose them. Alice doesn't really love them either. Slowly, the house and its contents become hated as they lose their ability to dampen the lingering force of the thwarted dreams. And as the old yearnings begin to gather strength inside, Alice and Mike feel lonely and abandoned, each perhaps even a bit betrayed by the other. Each suspects that the other forced him to sacrifice the dream.

The house that once served as their solace has now become a source of pain, a reminder that they were cheated. What Mike and Alice do not realize is that they cheated themselves. They pretended for so long to enjoy what they were doing that they believed it. Now they can't understand why they don't like the things they pretended to like. Or that they never liked them so much in the first place. In the beginning they loved themselves and their potential for what they would be. Because they were unable to develop their promise, they find themselves less fulfilled and now find it difficult to love anything.

The house they built to quell their original feelings of defeat has taken over their lives and conspires to limit them, to rob them of the chance of real fulfillment, the chance of ever being happy.

At the moment Mike can only see the symbols of what he will lose if he changes. He is panicked that his world might lack meaning if he were without them. He has forgotten how much his dream to be an architect meant. Alice and Mike are quick to tell you how much they love their children and how much joy they get from them, but even parenthood is not as they originally planned it. They had once hoped that they would go away with the children for long periods of time, maybe another country for a year, or to have long vacations and travel together, spend time together and get to know them better and share growing up.

They wanted to do a lot more with the children than they did, but things just kept piling up. Projects at Mike's office need to be finished. Meetings, appointments, duties, obligations, relatives, parties, friends, neighbors, and pets need to be taken care of. They don't have time for anything else. The system had done its work. They don't think about their dreams. At least not very much.

Why did they do it? Alice had been very good in dance in high school and college, but she wasn't outstanding and never was seriously considered at her auditions for dance companies. She was pleasant, enthusiastic and had a certain stage presence and style. She realized that she would never be good enough to be a star, but she continued to believe that with a little more effort she could join a troupe and work regularly.

That would take time and dedication. To dance, to perform at anything, one must make it the central point in one's life. It must come first. There must be a daily time set aside only for practice. After Alice's marriage, these plans were given up on the surface because they did not seem feasible financially. That's how Alice put it. In truth she could have danced after she got married if she had really wanted to. But being away from people in dance, made it more difficult to maintain an interest at the same level as before. The old doubts, the memories of being rejected for not being good enough, haunted her.

If Alice had thought about it carefully, she would have seen that she had more time after marriage to work at dancing. She could have organized her day so that the housework would be done on a schedule. The rest of each day she could have done her exercises and danced. But she did not see it this way and gradually allowed housework and small details to fill her life. Although Alice was not aware at the time, she was *threatened* by the possibility of having more time to practice. Given the freedom to develop, she would no longer have as good an excuse for not succeeding. If she could really be good, it would show in time. If she did try and did not get ahead, then she would have a hard time consoling herself.

She had been rejected before. She remembered that.

The fear of commitment is not the fear of hard work. It is the fear of being rejected where one feels most involved. Ideally, the dedication needed for success at anything should be ingrained as part of a discipline started when someone is quite young. Then the work becomes part of the way one expresses feelings. It becomes a world under complete control when the rest of the world is going mad. It is the microcosm you can run to when you need to be with yourself. People who build their own world in this way accept themselves more and are more able to feel satisfied.

Most of us are committed to denying our dreams and adapting to an expected, established form of behavior as players in someone else's world. Because Mike found that he would not be able to go on to graduate school and still wanted to marry Alice after graduation, he went to work in engineering. Maybe he felt that Alice would not wait for him if he finished graduate school. And he did have some doubts about his abilities in architecture and wasn't really sure whether or not he wanted to venture that far.

Alice and Mike got married before either of them knew themselves or had the chance to come to terms with their dreams. They did not know whether their dreams were real or imagined, worth following or simply folly. The opportunity to test out what they felt about themselves was avoided and they entered a commitment to each other which demanded constancy in a given role. This inhibited growth and prevented them from finding who each of them really was. Their life perpetuated their need to maintain commitments and hid their dreams from them.

Alice and Mike substituted commitments for their ideals. When they feel that life is empty and get upset, they look outside themselves—which is where they have always looked for answers. All they see outside is their fulfilled commitments. Inside they still feel unfulfilled. They don't understand how they can be doing everything that is expected of them and still feel empty.

How can they possibly change? They would have to give up the possessions to which they have grown accustomed and which they believe sustain them. If they do try to change, they must finally test their own dreams, the very thing they avoided when they first got caught in the spiral that now chokes them. If they do try, there is the possibility that they will fail just as before. In fact, it may even be harder for them to succeed now because they have less time and energy to give. But it is possible to get out of the trap and succeed. Alice can open up a dance studio, get back into condition and dance. And Mike can start again. He still has friends in the construction business who remember the designs he did for them when he was only in high school. It could happen.

Why don't people change? Why do they spend their lives doing what they really dislike? To begin with, you must admit that you are unhappy where you are. This is very difficult to do, if only because it means conceding that what one has done to this point seems to some extent without meaning. This is not to say that the years of bringing up a family, working and (hopefully) saving have not been for a good purpose. Rather, it means that the work was made tolerable primarily because it fulfilled an obligation, not because it had a special meaning in and of itself.

Some people are not aware of the conditions under which they work. This sounds incredible, but many people who work in situations that are extremely uncomfortable or without emotional reward learn to shut out their world to the point where it no longer bothers them. They allow themselves to become much like machines. If a person isn't aware of the world around him, he finds no need to change. He will just keep on going on at what he is doing until he drops in his tracks.

Change is most likely to occur when a person realizes that what he wants is not available where he presently is. He must recognize that he has not been doing what he wants in life. He must tolerate feeling some hurt over being unfulfilled. He must concede that he still wants more and is willing to risk something for it. Discontent must precede adventure.

Millions of people are not pleased with the state of their hopes about their role, career, place in society and it's a fact that they have little to make them feel that things will get better. Why don't they change?

The answer is complicated yet obvious. Most people are like Mike and Alice: they build huge symbols (homes, etc.) to consume time and effort. They displace their feelings and invest them in these symbols. Material symbols help to make society stable because they help people to think less. It's the individuals in the society who are the losers. Like Mike and Alice, they become lost in the symbols, rather than in themselves. In part, these symbols are useful. They do bring pleasure and for some people they represent all the goals that are needed for fulfillment. Often when such people get upset about a symbol they change it, not their way of life.

A job that is outside one's area of interest is just another symbol. What most people call change is merely the exchanging of one symbol for another. A person gives up one boring job for another or moves from one house to another. In the end he is likely to be in much the same position as before. There is very little change in his life style.

Why should this be so? People switch symbols (rather than really change) because they are afraid. Their fears are varied indeed. Besides the financial fears mentioned before, there is the fear of moving to a strange area after a long time in one location. The fear of disappointing others is also strong. And many people become whatever they are simply because it was expected of them.

Everyone tries to please someone, and usually begins by trying to please one's parents. It is very difficult for some people to become their own masters and to feel good about something merely because it pleases them. They feel a lack of direction and they make up for it by reacting to some other figure in authority whom they try to please.

These people are often miserable much of their lives. People who grow up this way often had parents who were not easy to please or who were stingy in giving praise. As a result, these people continue their struggle by seeking out a boss who is also difficult to please and by trying to win praise from him.

Much of our work just consumes time. Even if it seems ridiculous, childish and sometimes demeaning, we do it because it is expected of us. Hours are wasted on telephone calls and memos and correcting minor misunderstandings between people. Energies are sapped by backbiting, envy and complaining. Business and club meetings often serve little purpose other than to allow the people who run them to control other people or play teacher, boss or person-in-power. These gatherings rarely accomplish enough to justify the time they waste. Most creative activity gets done away from "work" because the rigidity of the business world often makes it impossible to implement new ideas. Frustration builds.

It is as if a little policeman inside us is ruling our actions and holding us back. The policeman feels pleased when we comply. We feel guilty or defeated. These inhibitions are often difficult to overcome, and they are among the reasons why people do not break away to do what they want. The little policeman will have none of it. This is a very powerful force and should never be underestimated. If someone decided to give up all of his material possessions he would still have to contend with his inhibitions.

Before making a change in one's life one must come to terms with one's family. Husbands often accuse their wives of holding them back by being tied down to the house and children, by not being adventuresome. Well, wives were either that way when their husbands married them in the first place or they were shaped that way by mutual consent, like Mike and Alice.

The fact is you get what you ask for. It's likely that if a wife whose role had always been to resist her husband suddenly agreed to change, the husband would feel threatened. Without going into long psychiatric explanations, people generally marry people they feel safe with. Some people are impulsive and need the controls of an opposite type, someone who keeps them in line. Ideally, both parties in a marriage should be able to control themselves and their own feelings and still be able to be spontaneous, independently of the spouse. No marriage is ideal and people often get cast into roles by the other. The roles people play often represent qualities that the spouse lacks. In fact, the willingness to assume the needed role is often the reason why people marry each other.

When two such roles complement each other it can make for pleasant, stable marriages. It also makes it more difficult for a partner to change. As two people live together they become dependent on the other person's style of action and use it to manage their own feelings. Inevitably, there is great resistance when a partner moves out of his role.

Richard, for example, is very impulsive and frequently comes home with wild ideas for making money. He is routinely put down by his wife, Patricia, who wants to stay where she is. Before his marriage, Richard accomplished little because he was never able to stay with one idea. Much of Richard's success comes from the stability which Patricia offers him. If Patricia agreed to go along with one of his impulsive ideas, he would feel unsure of himself because he depends upon her attitude to keep him on a straight path.

Such couples are not doomed to stay the same way

forever. It is possible for them to change without breaking up. Even those couples who depend highly upon each inhibiting the other can grow if they share their feelings about their new plans. Difficulties arise when a decision to initiate or to resist change is made with no room for discussion.

People who depend on a partner not to change his role have even more to fear than his change. They fear that if the marriage dissolves they would themselves dissolve—fall apart. They believe that it may be less painful in the long run to endure an uncomfortable situation at home than to risk making a change and inviting chaos. Yet even when two people are fairly set in their ways growth is possible, providing the partners are willing to tolerate some discomfort. Growth involves a rearranging of values, and it is often difficult in the beginning to agree on what is most important. Real discussion is essential. Without it there can be no agreement. And without agreement, growth together is limited.

The main reason why you may not make a meaningful change in your life this year is that you probably don't really look at what your needs are. Instead, you look at symbols and deal with them. Painting the house is just not going to make your wife feel better if she really wants to run her own dance studio. Changing engineering firms is not very helpful if you really want to be an architect.

In situations where a husband sees his wife as the major obstacle to the fulfillment of his life's dream, it is common to find that he had previously expected the wife to act this way. Years ago, when he was less sure of himself, he married her knowing she would not let him venture into strange and difficult areas. He could claim that his failures were the result of trying to please her. If he does get the chance to move and feels strong enough to do so, he is faced with the problem of helping his wife make an adjustment to his new attitudes, for now he is more willing to oppose her.

On the other side of the fence, some women find it easier to allow their husbands to dominate them than to assume responsibility for their own lives. Others become involved in housewifery as a way of keeping from doing what they want and avoiding self-confrontation.

Being a mother and housewife is time-consuming and rough, but it isn't that rough. It's a rare woman who could not cut her housework significantly without really upsetting anyone. The difficulty is that the entire housewife routine has become a ritual for many women. Without it they would feel lost.

Perhaps you want to break loose, but you have managed to plan your routine so it swamps you. Well, you can change it! Spacing children so they are born just at the time when you might become a little freer may mean that you are looking for a new reason to stay home. But remember: the child who becomes the reason why mother never finds herself has to bear a real burden. You have to find your own meaning in life.

Okay, so now you've done it. You've made a schedule and organized your days better. Now you've got all this free time. You can do anything you want. Don't turn on the television! Television is bad for you. Now you can go and tell your friends that you read a psychiatrist's book that said television is bad for you. What else are you going to do with all your free time? You can go looking into the museums and shops, but be careful or you'll fall into another rut.

Let's suppose that you do decide to get out to do something you've always wanted. And you find something you really love. Suddenly, without warning, sparks are flying. Your husband is making little comments about your new activities, your judo class, your painting or your job. He may be very subtle about it. Subtle! Ha! You may hear little comments like, "While you were out Cindy woke up and started crying and wouldn't go back to bed without a kiss from you." Who needs to hear that? What does your husband think you are? Another sample: "I tried and tried, but I couldn't fry the eggs the way you do, and the kids just wouldn't eat them. So I yelled at them and they refused to eat anything." It's the same thing. Can you believe this guy? What is he trying to do?

He thinks he's helping. He is saying that you are so special that it's impossible for him even to attempt to replace you in the house and the kitchen. And in some way you have to take the blame for his nonsense. Before, when you were ambivalent about working outside the house, you tried to rationalize that what you were doing at home was special. Come on, look at it, you pat yourself on the shoulder all the time! Listen to yourself: "No one makes hot dogs like Mummie." What does it take to make a hot dog? You've got everyone believing you've got the special touch and are irreplaceable. Maybe your love and care are special and are needed, even irreplaceable, but not for twenty-four hours a day, 365 days a year!

You needed to feel *that* special to placate your old fears that any fool could take over your duties. The trouble is that part of you still believes that you are truly irreplaceable. Take my word for it: if you had a houseful of servants and never even buttered your kids' bread, let alone cut off the crusts from the toast (because *your* kids don't eat crusts), your kids wouldn't think much differently of you than they do now. You can give the kids all they need in much less time. The only one who believes your performance is an act of love is you. And even you don't really believe it.

If you feel as if you're in a prison, it is probably one of your own making, and you must be the one to break it down.

If your family does begin to help out at home to give you more time but does so in ways different from your own, just accept it. If you go around the house with a sponge, cleaning up after everyone when they say they have already cleaned up, they'll just be undermined and will eventually leave all the cleaning to you. Why should they bother if you are going to do it anyway? You have to give up your image of being everything to everyone. *You have to be something to yourself.*

The hardest thing for a woman to overcome is her own stereotyped view of her role in the home. Motherhood is great, but there's no need to push it to the point where everything you do in the home is sacred. Do you really believe that no one opens up a jar of peanut butter like you can? Well, your kids don't believe it either. The reason why they squawk when you're not there is often not even related to your role as a mother. It's just because you're not there. Kids get that way when their teacher leaves the room. Why should they react differently when you're not home? Oh, I almost forgot. You have to feel that you're different so you can stand your life.

If you hope to succeed, you must overcome your husband's resistance to your new image. He is really very angry at you for all your independence. First, it upsets his schedule. He wants his life to be easy to manage. He doesn't like to be bothered with the children's nonsense. He can barely stand his own nonsense, and his boss all day. The fact of the matter is that he *is* angry at you, and he will use as many ways of showing this as possible. You'll hear little digs at the new people in your life.

Why is he doing this? He's supposed to love, honor, cherish, care for and support you. Why is he such a problem?

First, many men, not all fortunately, feel uncomfortable about their wives working, especially if their wife's contribution significantly improves the way they live. This may sound silly and contradictory, but it really is not. The man's traditional role as the great provider is not as believable as it once was. Some men need to be believed in, in this way, just as some women have to be thought of as the great mothers they see themselves. Even though I have it from good sources that they all scream at their kids a lot.

Men are just as likely to be in the same unhappy, unsatisfying position in their lives as women are in the home. They would like to be doing something else, but their obligations hold them down. A wife's starting to work may seem to imply that the man's obligations are not completely met and may be taken by the husband as an insult. The husband feels his efforts aren't good enough. Men may think also that their sacrificing is not worth it. Fortunately, these attitudes can be overcome by understanding the feelings behind them and discussing them together.

There is another hidden threat when a wife begins to bring home enough money. The husband may feel that it is now feasible for him to relinquish some of his financial obligations and go out and find himself. Good news? Not always. The husband may also regard it as a threat because it forces him to put up or shut up regarding his dream. The net result of all this is that the husband gets angry at the wife.

It is remarkable that more women do not break away from the home. There are just as many skilled, intelligent, well-educated women as men. To reduce an eager, bright human being to living in a world of children under three feet high must have its limits, its breaking point somewhere.

Husbands don't understand this. They only express how hard it must be but don't improve the situation by helping their wives develop a life of their own. One of their fears is obvious: the wife might find a new sexual partner. Most of the objections against wives working are at least partly grounded in this fear, whether he admits it or not. It is only natural to feel this way. But even if there are sexual overtones in the wife's decision to become more independent there is no reason why she should reverse that decision. Overtones do not mean activity. To curtail the search for one's self because you are afraid of what you may find is worse than not looking at all. Anyway, why should husbands judge their wives by their own feelings toward the women at their own office? And why should husbands feel that only they should be exposed to the temptations of an office Christmas party?

The greatest hindrance to changing the way you live this year is probably the way you have rationalized your role in life. And this includes more than the way you make hot dogs. In order to tolerate menial tasks, people have a way of making what they do seem more involved than it really is. Everyone does this to point out that he is special and clever. Everyone wants to feel unique.

There is a difference between feeling special to someone else (a spouse or child) and being able to do things in a unique way, like designing a dress or singing a song. Not only is most of what every ordinary person does very close to busy-work. This is true of everyone, including the President, generals, and leaders in education, medicine, publishing, finance—everyone. Everyone likes to think of himself as a decision maker, vitally important to the outcome of things. Yet in most respects all of us are replaceable in the roles we play. Only in the sense that we are special to another person are we irreplaceable, unless we are blessed with a unique talent, or can express ourselves uniquely in our work.

Most of us do feel that we are special to another person, but few feel that we possess a talent or a special view of the world that makes us unique and memorable. Nevertheless, it is a fact that everyone does have something within him that makes him different, unique. It is up to each of us to find out this special gift and to develop it to the greatest degree possible.

This is difficult to do, not only for the reasons I have been discussing but also because few of us have enough confidence in our own worth to try. We need someone to encourage us, to tell us that we can start a business of our own or write well, sing well, or make a jelly worth mass marketing. We become vulnerable in the face of possible criticism if we take that big step toward our true selves.

This happens because when we do our own thing, we impart our personality to it. We touch the world, make our own presence known and open to possible rejection. If we are successful, we seem that much more real to ourselves and our world makes that much more sense. If not, there are ways to overcome the feelings of personal defeat.

To admit that you need something else in life is probably the first step in getting free. It is also to admit that your life has not been as satisfying as you pretended. Why protest that "No one can be happy all of the time"? It's a poor excuse! There *are* people who are happy, who are doing things that make them feel special. To construct a world of obstacles to fill your life, drain your energy and make you feel guilty when you feel like leaving seems a great waste indeed.

To waste one's life is to waste the entire world.

4

EXCUSES, EXCUSES

Responsibility! The word has a solid ring to it. Let me say it again: responsibility. You know, it even *sounds* responsible. Just *saying* the word "responsibility" makes a person seem responsible. "I know it's my responsibility to work five days a week." That sounds very grown up. It makes whoever says it seem as if he works five days a week. Even if he doesn't.

Responsible! Responsible is what lawyers try to get the other party to be when there's an accident, what bosses try to make an underling appear when a deal falls through. But if *you* are responsible for something, it means that it is within your power to change or alter it. Not until you accept responsibility for your own life can you change it.

Responsibility, the sum total of all the obligations we feel or imagine, comes like the ghost of Christmas past to haunt us when we want to run away from duty. Usually, the best course of action is not running away from one's duty and obligations. People should fulfill their obligations and their duties to the best of their ability. But, before he consents to be governed by them, a person should determine what his duties and obligations are. To become the slave of obligations that have little relevance to your needs or feelings is to be concerned only with appearances, with the way you think you should be, not the way you are.

One does owe much to other people. Children do need to be loved, supported and fed. It is almost impossible to list all the obligations that accumulate over the years. Beyond the few basic necessities, dozens of demands seem to have grown and taken over your life; going to meetings, acting as committeeman, running errands, making deliveries, often for other people who could just as well have done it themselves. Somewhere in your schedule bursting with obligations you have lost sight of the person you once wanted to be. Your commitment to your potential to be special has been replaced by errands and busywork that you could well do without. And what is your place in all this churning?

There is nothing wrong with doing something purely and solely for you and no one else. It's okay to be selfish some of the time. After all, you only have one life to do what you want. Whatever you feel guilty about when it comes to doing for yourself probably isn't all that selfish. If you are fulfilling other people's needs most of the time, what's wrong with doing something for yourself once in a while? I have never seen anyone hang a sign on an office door, "Gone Fishing for the Afternoon." And I don't see why someone doesn't. Everyone has to go fishing some time. What's wrong with living the life you want to live? What's wrong with thinking of you?

Much of the time we do things because we are too unsure of ourselves to say, "No" or too afraid of appearances to risk being different by refusing. We became swallowed up in commitments to other people before we really understood that we *could* say "No" and that saying "No" does not imply something evil about us. We also have rights. If anyone treats us unequally, it is most often ourselves.

Many times each year in grammar school class elections, children lose by the one vote that they themselves have cast for their opponent. They did not feel right about voting for themselves. Children do this all the time and let opportunities pass by, too unsure of themselves to take advantage of them. Many of us have not outgrown this kind of thinking. Although we hate losing, we don't feel right about voting for ourselves. It is rarely others who take our rights away.

People who have their rights taken away have often already yielded them in spirit.

When we act because of a sense of duty that is out of touch with our feelings or needs, we only lose time in the search for ourselves. Few of those chores done purely out of obligation pay dividends in personal pleasure. They only create an image in the minds of others that we are dutiful or just dull. If carrying out such duty leaves no time to do what you want, then it is very destructive. After a while the swallowed resentment toward others begins to build and will surface, quite possibly whenever it is least welcome. It usually makes itself known in embarrassing or hurtful ways, sometimes injuring the very person for whom you were making sacrifices.

Karl had stuck to a job even though he referred to it for years as "my sentence." He became more and more irritable at home and less and less fun to be with, but he did not consider changing jobs, taking real vacations or even pursuing a hobby that he could call his own. Everything

Karl did was to insure that his son would have an education so that the boy would not be trapped as Karl was. During the son's final year at college, Karl became so argumentative and downright nasty at work that he was eventually let go, causing great financial hardship and placing his son's education in jeopardy. Karl had really been angry at his own son all along for having everything that Karl wanted for himself. Finally, the anger had boiled up to the surface and Karl deflected it against his co-workers at the office. If Karl had thought of himself, this crisis could have been avoided.

To live for the sake of appearances can be as addictive as taking drugs. It takes a lot of energy to keep up with the Joneses (who probably couldn't care less). Often there is little strength left to do your own thing for yourself. More and more, it's other people who supply you with your reasons for doing whatever you feel you must. And you duck the idea of making a change for fear of what others might think of you.

And who are these "others?" If you look around you to count the people you can trust and entrust and if you find more than five, you are either very unusual or a terrific liar. So whom are you trying to please and why?

Many of us have become what David Riesman described as "other-directed." We do things because of forces outside ourselves, not because of our own internal needs and values. We gradually begin to approach the situation described by Bertrand Russell: "Everything is done for the sake of something else and not for its own sake." At this point it becomes difficult to distinguish for whom we are doing what.

Regardless of what people say to the contrary, most of

us do not care very much about what others think or feel. To care means to value the feelings of others as highly as your own. People usually base their judgments about others on a few incomplete facts that are often highly distorted. What people decide about others depends very much upon their own mental processes, their needs and biases.

Almost everybody suffers from a form of psychological censorship that allows them to see only part of what goes on between themselves and others. We all distort our surroundings to some extent. No two people see the world (or even a minor car accident) alike.

The final impression and opinion that others form about you depends more upon who they are than upon what you do. Your actions are really explainable only to a few people, the small handful you trust. If they are good friends, they will understand. If they do not, you are alone in your decisions. But don't waste your time trying to keep up appearances for people who really do not care.

You are judged not by your actions alone but by what they mean to others. If you want to work while your children are at school, there will always be someone criticizing you for not being a good mother. Being a good mother in the eyes of such a person obviously means to be available every moment of every day whether or not your children need you. These people criticize you not for what you do, but for what your actions symbolize to *them*. Perhaps the critic had a mother who was not available when she was needed and still feels angry about it. Some parents deal with these angry feelings later in life by becoming slavishly attached to their own children and critical toward others who, in the critics' biased view, are less "loving." It's wise to keep in mind that criticism from such people often grows out of anger that they felt toward their own parent(s); they simply displace their anger on you. In various ways, the process of symbolic displacement colors many people's opinions of you. Look: you have your own problems. You don't need to spend your life trying to figure out how to please someone else. In some cases it's impossible.

When you fulfill your duty for fear of disapproval from others, your fear is probably not based on what you think of yourself but on what you think others think. How's that again? It's quite simple once you reflect about it. If you are speeding in your car and happen to pass a police car, you will falsely attribute to the policeman all sorts of ideas that he doesn't have. When you do this, you are giving expression to nothing but your very own fears. Unless you are being really reckless, he won't even notice you. Yet you will drive very cautiously, checking the rear view mirror, wondering what he will do. He couldn't really care less about you. You are the one who feels guilty.

We all invent our own policemen to control our wishes. Conformity for the sake of approval or duty is one of the toughest cops on patrol. He has to be big and tough because he contains the prohibitions against doing what we want to do, what we would do if no one were watching. And there isn't a single prohibition that we either didn't consent to or put up ourselves!

Just a minute! If we put all those prohibitions there in the first place, inventing them ourselves, then there really is no one to stop us from doing what we want. But there is us, unfortunately—the people who put up the prohibitions in the first place. Each of us is his own policeman. But his power works both ways. Because he has the power to restrict, he also has the power to sanction, to set you free.

No excuse is offered as regularly or loudly as "obligations to the family." People say, "If I left the job, we'd be all upset at home," or "I'd like to, but my wife wouldn't feel comfortable about it," or "The family needs me too much." In fact, presenting these statements like this may even seem a bit callous. I can hear readers saying, "You're not kidding! Everyone in my house would be plenty upset! That's exactly why I'm not making a move just now." Of course you are right: a move might make people upset. No matter what you do, no matter how small a change you make, someone is going to get upset. But to use this fact as the main reason for not doing anything about your life means that you're giving excessive importance to the obvious.

If you stay where you are but really want to do something else, yet you use the excuse that other people would be upset, then you are really doing nothing more than putting the blame on them. You aren't being self-sacrificing for their sake. You are using them as excuses for your own inaction and displacing your own fears about yourself (and possible failure) upon them. That's no way to live, is it? There is no excuse in the entire world big enough to keep you from doing what you really want to do. And no excuse is too small to keep you from doing something you don't want. How big your excuse is depends on how big you need it to be.

Denying oneself "for the sake of the children" is another favorite copout, and this one carries subtle consequences. I've already mentioned the mother who expands her work to fill up her time and then calls her efforts self-sacrifice for the family. Now let's look at what happens when you hide behind all this work because you're afraid to try out a new identity or new career.

If you spend all your time with housework you can't make anyone in the house believe you like it. They all know that you hate running around cleaning up after them. They don't really appreciate how hard you work at it. Why should they? Think for a minute: how many times have you had to shout and scold about keeping clean and orderly? How many times have you made the children feel ashamed or guilty over making a mess? If this were really the role in life you loved, you would be much more cheerful about it.

The homebody role calls for you to be patient and understanding. You are supposed to know intuitively that children make messes, that a husband is unable to make a sandwich without using six plates, that everyone leaves the cupboards open, as well as the drawers, that no one else seems to know how to open the dishwasher, let alone turn it on. This should be second nature to you—if you were really accepting of your role as a housewife.

No one expects you to love every single minute of this enterprise since it is mostly drudgery in pleasant, if somewhat noisy and disorganized surroundings. But you should be able to come to terms with it and accept it for what it is. It's all right to resent doing housework because it is drudgery. It's not all right to resent the people you claim you are doing it for, not if it keeps you from being where you'd rather be or doing what you really want.

Remember: if you really wanted to, you could rearrange your schedule, hire a baby sitter, get a job, and be free much of the time. If your answer is that you have little children, I can understand your reasoning; little children need attention. But if you feel resentful of them, I have very little sympathy for you. Because if you feel resentful now, you probably already see your children standing in your way and are using that as an excuse. Unless you do something about it you are unlikely to change this way of thinking, even when the children get older, because if you need an excuse now, you'll need one then, too. You must face the fact that you are afraid of something in yourself and that you fear change.

The children really have very little to do with keeping you back. During the years when you have to stay at home you could be doing a great deal of preparation for later. If you plan on having two or three children and space them every two years and you would like to begin doing something when the youngest is three or four, you have almost eight years to prepare. During that time you could sign up for night courses. You could get reading lists in the fields that interest you. During days when you find time (and since you will have a purpose, you will find time) you can read, consider and think about your plans.

What if you don't have a special interest? Should you give it all up and turn on television? So many women do and rob themselves of life's best opportunity to grow. You should inquire into local adult education programs and see what is available for study. You have all the time in the world, really. If you plan to read two hours a day you could finish several years of college work in those eight years. You can afford to experiment, to look into activities that have always interested you or that are just fun. Now is a good time to find an interest, to decide what skills you'll need and then to acquire them gradually. The years of child-rearing could be a period of self-rearing as well.

Children who grow up in a home where the mother is saying, in effect, "I'm only thinking of them" often feel resented and guilty. It becomes increasingly difficult to see mother as truly self-sacrificing when they understand how many of her troubles she creates herself as a way of making herself feel needed. They don't believe mother did it all for them even though mother says she did. Instead, they feel that they are really not worth all of mother's efforts. They feel guilty for making her kill herself.

This image of a mother knocking herself out to please them is one that they grow to hate. When she is sincere, the caring and the giving are sources of great pleasure and sustenance. A mother's insincere giving only produces a strong wish in the children to get out of the house as soon as possible. The children want to be free. Not free so they can do what they really want; just free of the overbearing sense of guilt and obligation and low self-esteem that this kind of a mother makes them feel. Kids get the message very clearly. The message is that mother is not doing this for them; she is doing it for herself, or so they won't know she's angry with them.

I am not knocking motherhood. I am only knocking the abuse of motherhood by some mothers. And they are not abusing motherhood as much as they are destroying their own chances to be happy and free.

If the evils that mothers perpetrate upon their children are upsetting, at least they are usually out in the open. Fathers who feel kept back because of their responsibilities to the children are just as bad. Often they're worse and less open about their feelings. When mothers act in a way that produces guilt they often do so by being a super-mother. When fathers feel frustrated in their lives it is harder to tell what is going on.

The father who feels he cannot change his life situation because of his children often expects them to be grateful for what he has given them. The children's social and educational opportunities are often talked about in a guilt-producing way: "Why do you think we live in such an expensive neighborhood? Why do I have to put so much money away? It's all for you!" The truth is otherwise. It's all because of *him*—father. It makes him proud to be able to afford it. At least it used to.

Unquestionably the material advantages *are* wanted for the children, too. The idea of giving your kids a better life than the one you had is an old American standby. Unfortunately, it is not a very accurate reflection of why parents really do what they do. The father who struggles to have a fine home for his kids is more likely struggling for the fine home he would like to have been brought up in himself. His kids have little to do with it. If he and his wife were childless, would they live in a place less nice? Almost certainly not.

Other customs also reveal the fallacy that fathers do things for their kids purely because they want them to have what the parents lacked. Just look at fathers buying toys that are too expensive and somewhat inappropriate for their sons at Christmas time—like a train set for a one-year-old. Is there any doubt who these toys are for? What makes people feel so awkward if they indulge themselves in what they want? Why can't a person say, "I never had that before, and I am going to get it for myself?" Why is it necessary to concoct a whole way of thinking, the myth that one is doing it for the sake of one's children, that it's alright to be indulgent to the kids, but not to oneself? Children resent gifts that are supposedly for them when they are really for the parents. It's a confused or an unusually greedy child who doesn't see through these weak protestations, who doesn't know what the adults are up to.

Very few children want to move to unfamiliar—if expensive—surroundings, no matter how bad things were at the old place. They prefer their friends and hiding places. If the children were consulted, they would vote to stay put. They are home. It's the parents who move for their own reasons and the parents overrule their children.

When such parents suggest a career for their children, their old, unfulfilled dreams seem to come alive again. They wish for their children what they once wished for themselves and couldn't have. For the son, good money and respect in the eyes of his fellowmen would be just right, perhaps in medicine. For the daughter it should be something that would enable her to remain independent and have a worthwhile interest of her own, maybe in education.

No question about it: much of what these parents want for their youngsters would never even come up for discussion if the mothers and fathers had had an opportunity to try out their dreams when they were young. If they had tested these dreams, any number of parents would have rejected the very career that they'd like to foist upon their children. These parents want their children to succeed to bolster their own lagging self-esteem, to set right their own unhappy settlement with the world. A child's success becomes justification for the parents' self-denial, proof that the parents could have succeeded if only they had had the same opportunities. It rarely occurs to them that if they can now afford to make these advantages available to their children, it may finally be possible to have many of these opportunities themselves. Certainly they are older and have lost much time. But their desire, determination, maturity, and ability to provide what they once lacked could tip the scales in their favor.

What do you suppose a child will think and do if he believes that just the fact of his being born has kept you from finding yourself and being happy? I'll tell you. He will either feel terribly guilty and see himself as worthless or, more likely, he will find it necessary to discredit your opinions. Eventually he'll see you as a poor slob who just didn't know what he was talking about or who had no courage.

You wouldn't want him to feel that way about your opinions and advice. You want to help him use his opportunities even if you don't like the way he uses them. After all, you don't always like the way you used your own opportunities, even if you believe they were small. Your children do not believe your excuse for not finding yourself.

Neither should you.

Here's another popular excuse: some people believe that if they had only had the opportunity they would be doing what they wanted long ago. Not true! It's just not true. I don't care how much you protest that you didn't have the opportunity. It just is not true. Don't say that times were different, that no one knew how to find work, let alone pay for an education. There are people who were in the same situation as you and who became successful even though they had no more than you. You probably call them "lucky," but that's rarely the story. Opportunity is usually available to everybody. What fluctuates is the amount of effort needed to take advantage of it. When you put off striving for new goals for yourself because you believe your opportunity has passed, you are only missing the opportunities that are *now* available. You still have time to do what you want.

Self-denial involves a twisted sense of duty and obligation. It has to be thankless. Look at it this way: you put off doing what you really want. You give to the children. Then you make them feel uneasy and sometimes guilty for having what you didn't. Maybe you'll sacrifice a vacation so they can have enough spending money in college. That is foolish. It can paralyze youngsters with guilt and ambivalence. How can they enjoy themselves or take full advantage of their opportunities, knowing you wanted to take that trip?

When you break plans you have long wished for, even when it's for people you love, you feel a loss and resentment. It's just part of being human. You don't need to apologize for it. You don't even need to give up that trip. Your kids would feel less resented, less guilty and better able to work if you took it. And they would learn that they have to earn money if later they want to take trips themselves.

You *can* learn to get more out of life by putting less in if you begin and take the first step: allow yourself to take something out. Some people just don't take anything out of life. No matter how much they put in, they never seem to enjoy anything. This only teaches others that working hard gets you nothing. The best thing you can do for your children is to show them that you know how to be happy and to enjoy what you have worked for. If you don't, you'll either make them feel pessimistic about life or that they must reject your example of hard work. Do you want to turn your child into a hippie? If you don't, you'd better start enjoying yourself, live more of your life for you and allow them to lead their life for them.

If you insist that your children prove themselves by going to college just because you didn't have the chance, or that they find a particular career because the time wasn't right for yours, you put your children in the same position that you were in. They won't be free to choose either.

Money can not only be as much of a disadvantage as poverty; it may also be irrelevant. The important resources are the emotional and intellectual endowments of your children. These can be enhanced by better surroundings and education. But nothing expands a child's intellectual ability as much as being loved and appreciated for what he is, without the need to fulfill a legacy he doesn't understand; which, if it is forced upon him, he will come to resent; or, if he is lucky, abandon.

The key is direction. Where should these resources be focused? Unless you are in the musical Bach family, it is likely that everyone in yours will have his own ideas and wishes about what he wants and how he sees himself.

To make children feel guilty if they do not become what you had in mind is to limit them and force them off course. The mother who pressures her daughter into the career in writing that she herself had always wanted (when the daughter really doesn't, and her abilities are limited) may be setting the stage for her daughter's own disenchantment years from now. The daughter may find herself trapped in some humdrum area of writing, wishing to move ahead but secretly fearing (and with good cause) that she hasn't enough ability to move on. Even worse, she may begin to question her ability to succeed in general.

If your children do follow your advice, your real wish still won't be satisfied. Even if they do succeed, as happy as you will be for them, you will still be troubled by that same feeling of personal unfulfillment, no matter how deep you bury it. The problem is still you.

And the kids who have achieved so much—what about them? Some will be happy simply because they finally pleased you. Your kids may be terrific successes because of your influence. But if their choices were based upon the need to please you they may have lost some capacity to fulfill themselves for their own sake.

Just like you!

You didn't know you could inflict your problems on them by helping them succeed where you could not. It's an appalling irony. You can perpetuate your problem into another generation. So what's wrong with letting children find out for themselves who they are? I'm sure most people would answer, "Nothing." Still, secretly, many hang on to the wish to mold their children into something that satisfies them.

This is not to say that parents don't know best sometimes. They may. Yet choosing a career, telling kids what in life is best for them, even if the children ask for it, may not be at all helpful. If your child doesn't know what he wants, he has to go through the depression and struggle of self-confrontation to find out. By all means discuss it with him. But the answers must come from him. If they do not, he is likely to end up doing something that has nothing to do with who he is. Well, now you see both sides of the coin.

The point is that parents must stop giving the excuse that they are living for their kids. They aren't; they are living for themselves, but feel too guilty to admit it. I have to say it again: there is nothing wrong with doing something because you want to. To be happy, you must do what you feel. To do what you think you *ought* is folly. Really now: isn't it unrealistic to make your children fulfill dreams you once had, dreams you never seriously tested against reality and which, for all you know, you might have given up if you had tried to follow them?

You must follow your own dreams even if it seems too late to change much. Grandma Moses was 80 when she started painting! The reason why it *seems* too late to change has nothing to do with time. It has to do with the way you look at obligations you acquired over the years. And, as we have seen, these obligations, for the most part, developed because you wanted to be held back; you were afraid of what you might find.

It's a vicious circle. The excuses you give for not finding what you say you want were actually created by you to keep you from finding what you want.

There are specific stages in life when you consolidate ideas about yourself, choose a direction, develop new insights and goals. These are very important periods; how one chooses at each point determines how much one is going to get out of life and how happy one will be. People use many excuses at each stage to explain their choices. This pattern of excuses becomes more fixed over the years.

The idealistic visions of the adolescent have barely subsided when adulthood forces him to make decisions about a career and the future. This is a very difficult time, because the assuming of responsibility begins to loom. It casts a shadow over one's entire world. What you look back on today as the golden days of carefree youth are really a nightmare of disorganization and lack of direction. The reasons for making so many bad choices in your life can probably be found during this stage. You probably could no longer stand the confusion and aimlessness and chose to do something mostly to gain some direction, just to get the hell out of there. The indecision was just too uncomfortable.

This happens to many people. Considering the chaotic way in which many of us choose careers when we are young, it's remarkable that anyone is ever happy in later years. Most young people know little about their chosen careers at the time of launching. If they don't get brainwashed by prejudiced parents, their most influential sources of information are friends who know little more than they do themselves. Then judgments are made on the basis of these talks. Actually, these judgments are strongly colored by fantasies and hopes. The kids know only one thing for sure: they feel uncomfortable without a goal. Somehow they believe at seventeen that they should know what they should do the rest of their lives.

What have we done to these kids? We have given them a broad and largely useless education to prepare them for almost nothing they can feel proud of. It has imparted so little knowledge about the world to them that they do not really know what to expect when they go out into it. Although most of what they are taught is irrelevant to anything they now do or will ever do, they are chastised if they do not get good grades. Grades become the measure of their worth, and the worst of horrors is not being admitted to college. Yet most American colleges are of little help in solving this problem. The struggles in which we find ourselves embroiled for the rest of our lives—living in the world as it really is, coping with our thoughts and feelings—are rarely dealt with in "education."

It only pushes us ahead, teaching little and making increasingly difficult demands that are literally as well as figuratively academic. It's perfectly possible to acquire a higher degree and, at the same time, no useful abilities. The concept of apprenticeship at the hands of a master has been largely lost. Unless children are prodigies whose talents are so towering that they cannot be denied, they get a "well-rounded" education that may be no help with their most urgent task: self-discovery. Consequently, when they reach the age for decision-making about life, they confront the realization that they cannot *do* a blessed thing. This is the time for exploring the possibilities. Unhappily, our culture makes such a reconnaissance much too difficult.

Even though a youngster in a more "primitive" society who begins an apprenticeship at an early age may not know exactly what he wants to do later, he may be better off in the end than the average youngster in this country. This seeming paradox is not difficult to understand. When a youngster learns as an apprentice, he channels many of his feelings into his trade and uses his skills as a way of expressing them. He grows with his craft. Since it has become a vehicle of self-expression, he can be happy with his work in later years. He may discover other compatible careers later in life, but the skill he grew up with still serves to satisfy him.

The young adult in America may not develop the same ability to express feelings through his work.

We envy the special talent, the brilliant star who crosses the headlines and airways of our highly communicative world. Such a powerful figure, such opportunity, such victory! Why can't we follow our own talents and develop them even if they are not so well pronounced?

When they enter college, most young people know themselves only as a child to some parent and feel a certain way about it. They may know that success is expected of them, but their life experience is too meager to know where to try. A period of trying out dreams and identities usually begins in the early twenties. By their mid-twenties most people have gone through their first real confrontations with reality and usually their first compromises. They struggle to get ahead, achieve stability, and develop skills. When a strong need for money exists, it limits a consideration of alternative careers, which is important because changes are easiest during the early twenties.

At this time people begin to make sacrifices and tolerate unpleasant situations to get ahead. Goals are kept foremost in mind and self-indulgences are denied. During the late twenties people begin to feel fulfilled if they have been on the right track. The early efforts should be paying off by then, and if ability was there in the first place some success should be apparent.

Young people at this time are frequently comparing themselves and their position to what and where they think they should be. It is this continuous confrontation of their hopes with reality that is so characteristic of the twenties, makes them so exciting and at the same time so depressing.

No one finds life the way he wanted or expected, and this can cause a setback. Adjustments must be made. If people do not reconsider their goals and identities during these years they will find it increasingly difficult to make big changes. Instead, they find rationalizations for staying in a situation that doesn't suit them.

This is where unrest starts. Men become rats in the rat race. Young mothers, disenchanted with their loss of freedom, prisoners in their own homes, begin to rave about the baby and how wonderful everything is. They make their home the central point in their lives. This attitude alienates more women from their husbands than any other. Women begin to think of themselves as "very married," but even though they boast how wonderful marriage is, it doesn't relieve their discontent and resentment. This resentment goes underground to find expression in less easily identifiable forms of anger directed at the family: moodiness, sloppiness, chronic fatigue. The sweet "girl that I married" disappears. Somebody's short-tempered mother takes her place.

The thirtieth birthday, or the twenty-ninth, is a killer. They undermine the belief that there is enough time left to do anything. The pressure is on: what the hell *do* you want out of life? And how the hell are you going to get it? And where do you start?

> "Happy birthday to you,
> Happy birthday to you.
> You're running out of life expectancy
> Now what will you do?"

That's the song all right! I'd know it anywhere! At thirty people often do change jobs and sometimes go new ways, but usually the inheritance from the past crawls up and covers them with one of the hardest of all the great excuses to deal with:

"I can't change. I've invested so much time and effort. It's all I know. It's my whole life."

In essence, the clutch of turning thirty repeats itself throughout your life. At forty, forty-five, fifty, fifty-five, sixty, sixty-five. And at each of these times the only difference is that the music gets louder and the excuse "I've given so much time" gathers more support from more birthday candles and the swift passage of more years.

It may be true: you may have invested your whole life in becoming something. But it may also be true that whatever you invested in has little to do with who you are. You may still be trying to maintain the goals and view of yourself that you had when you were in your teens. You often don't trust your teenager's opinion. Why should you trust what you believed when *you* were nineteen? How do you know you were right? Maybe you've been wrong about yourself all along.

You can see through your kid's excuse. You may even get angry when you see part of yourself in him, especially when he uses the same excuses that you used to. Why is it you can't see through your own excuses?

We've looked at the excuses of keeping up appearances, obligations, and all the investments in time you have made. You know these excuses only hold water because you *say* they are solid enough to do so. They are entirely within your control. They are your way of handling and justifying to yourself your failures, cowardice and fear. *You* have chosen your life. You have decided to sit home all day and center your life about the kids or to stay as a rat in the rat race because you get more money.

You can also decide not to. In the following chapters I will discuss, step by step, how you can break out of any trap, but let's start to face the most drastic possible change right now. You can get a divorce.

"It's not fair to the children to get divorced," is an all-time favorite excuse. In free translation this means, "I feel guilty over being angry at the kids for making it so difficult to get divorced." The people who think divorce is unfair to the kids have never taken a poll of children who came from homes where there was a divorce. The only children who show a persistent strong desire for their parents to get back together are children with very passive or unrealistic needs—or characters in Walt Disney movies. When children say they would like their parents to stay together, they really mean that they wish the marriage worked better. Giving children hope for improvement when the marriage is clearly unsavable is only to give them grief. Children who hope for reconciliation in the face of an obviously bad marriage and do not alter their wish in spite of the years of deterioration have problems themselves, perhaps excessive dependence or an inability to cope with reality. Most children feel a sense of enormous relief when parents who have been carrying on a battle for years, even if in silence, finally decide to part ways.

No child ever gave parents a badge of merit for staying together just for his sake. Staying together for the sake of children constitutes one of the most unfair acts parents can inflict upon a child. There is nothing fair about staying married and creating an atmosphere that is not merely filled with hostility and resentment but creates much guilt in children. When these bad marriages later end up in divorce anyway, as they frequently do, a child often wrongly feels that he had some role in causing the split, which saddles him with even more guilt.

Children usually resent both parents for staying together in a bad marriage and not getting a divorce. This may sound completely alien to many readers, but it is so. Such parents often feel that their children should bless them for being so self-denying and staying together in continued disharmony while the children grow up, as if those years weren't complicated enough without the additional mixed emotions that such a deadlock generates. More likely than not, all the self-sacrificing required to stay together for the sake of children will be interpreted by the children not as helping them but as a hostile act on the parents' part.

Children in a marriage where things are going badly usually side with the parent whom they need most urgently at that time, not invariably with whoever they feel is "right" in the parental conflict. This is why young children will almost always side with the mother.

In general, however, children are very good at seeing what goes on, even if they are unable to put it into words. They resent what is happening and hate being used as an excuse. They would like everything to be fine again, but prefer a divided house, a separate peace, to war. It is very sad.

The children's wish for reconciliation is most strongly expressed at the beginning of marital difficulties. They hope that parents will make up. If the situation is allowed to persist for long, a tremendous amount of tension builds up and interferes with a child's ability to concentrate, study, have fun and grow. There no longer is any place where the child can go to find peace. He can say he has a father and a mother, but he has only tension with them.

I am sure that there are some people who find these past paragraphs horrifying and feel that a madman is writing them. I truly regret upsetting anyone, but if you have tried everything to work things out, have been unsuccessful, are thinking about divorce and find this extremely upsetting, you really owe it to yourself to take a look at the reasons why you and your spouse are staying together. What can a marriage be worth that *obligates* you to love? Doesn't it matter that the children also feel burdened and resent the pressure on both parents?

When situations like this develop, both parents are under such intense pressure that neither can muster energy and time to be a good parent. The children become doubly robbed. Not only do they lack a happy home, but they also lack a parent who is able to deal with them, at least not without some resentment for being an obstacle on the road to freedom. Believe me: children sense this no matter how well it is hidden.

In time such children will realize the futility of feeling guilty and will stop thinking that they are to blame for these marital difficulties. These children often begin to get into difficulty in their own lives when they start to resent the parents for cheating them for so long and for being used as a whipping boy.

The children begin to see their parents' marriage as empty and cold, offering little that they need. They have to deal with their doubts about being loved and wanted. Children coming from such a situation often find the lure of intense early relationships irresistible and may be attracted to people who are grossly inappropriate. They make choices impulsively. Rather than cope with their feelings about themselves they may seek solace in a relationship that imitates their parents' relationship or tries to make up for what it lacks.

Ruth was an attractive girl, the oldest of three children whose mother and father were continually battling each other. The father had a seductive manner with Ruth and was a runaround. Mother was cold and insensitive. Very little warm feeling was expressed toward the children at home. Because she was the oldest, Ruth got the least attention and was forced to look outside her home for it. At fifteen Ruth went to work, partly because she needed the money, but mostly because she felt that she simply had to get out of the house. It should not come as a surprise that she began to have an affair with her married boss who appreciated her and who himself was having difficulties with his wife who was also ungiving. While there were other factors in Ruth's personality that led her into such a situation, it was mainly the exposure to her parents' irreconcilable conflicts that drove her to seek a relief from pressure in her own way.

It is often said that the children from broken homes have emotional difficulties. They do have more problems than other children, but that is not because the marriage ended in divorce; it is rather that the marriage from which these children came was not a good one in the first place and that it lasted too long. Poor marriages do not stable children make. Poor marriages where the parents stay together "for the sake of the children" produce children who feel guilty, who come to resent it all later on and who are less stable than children from marriages which ended sooner.

* * *

Another common excuse that people offer for their failure to change is money. If you stayed in your present situation, would more money make you considerably more content? I very much doubt it. If you think that having more money would allow you to change, you may be right, but your chances of ever getting enough to convince you to leave are slim. Who do you know in the past year who has kept at the same job and made enough money to do what he really wanted? Probably no one. Unless you're expecting to inherit a million dollars next year, you'll have to change on your own.

Suppose you cut back on what you earn; or eliminate your second home; or don't buy a new car this year; or don't dine out as frequently. Would this make you miserable if you could do the things you really wanted? Only you can answer that. When one has a career one likes, a person one really loves, a microcosm to buffer the cold shocks of an uncaring world, a little world to control and make beautiful, the rest of the world seems to be manageable regardless of how little money is available. Without your own little world the going is rough no matter how much you have.

Now, take away all of these excuses for a moment and think. You will never really be truly happy or successful until you become you. The people you know who have been financially successful were most likely that way because they followed a personal quirk or individual way of doing things. They had a belief in themselves and in their way and fought for it. Perhaps they modified it so it worked better, but it was always a part of them. It came from within them in the first place. They didn't borrow it from their parents. It wasn't dictated by guilt. They became themselves and their work became the fulfillment of their needs. This is why, even though they may work harder than other people, they get pleasure out of working. To do *their* work is not work to them; it is to be themselves in a way that makes them feel most them. It is very difficult to become fatigued or bored when one is happy at work. On the contrary, output usually increases.

It's a shame that most people waste so much of their lives preoccupied with thoughts and wishes that are not expressed in what they do. Bank clerks dream of being in politics. Bakers wish for a boat to take to sea. Secretaries dream of living abroad. Lawyers long to be ski bums. Housewives dream their dreams of a place away from the peanut butter, of mornings without television waking them up, of a life where there is some time for themselves and their husbands together, and not just on vacations. These thoughts and fantasies are the expression of what you need to be content. To the extent that they are not fulfilled you will feel bored, tired, have headaches, upset stomachs, become tense and have difficulty sleeping because the role you play doesn't satisfy the real you.

So you spend your life looking for ways to relax. Your friends tell you to take up a hobby or a sport. That may help a great deal. But why can't life be spent doing whatever resolves tension rather than creates it? Even people who do live a life predominantly given over to self-expression feel tension, but this tension is directed at finding new ways of expressing their feelings in their work, not escaping from it.

You say it can't be done in our society? A person can't always find a way of living that's fulfilling? Then I say our society is wrong and is making nervous wrecks out of all of us. And I also don't believe you and your excuses. You should never stop heading for the life that suits you. You should never give up the search for yourself.

There is no real success in life until you do what fulfills you. Finding this takes time, but it is time well spent. Not to find it is surely to lose time, to watch each birthday pass as a reminder of opportunities lost forever.

To give up the excuses and find a place that is especially yours is to watch the passage of years, not like someone dreading the advance of a superior enemy across a darkening plain, but as a friend who leads you closer to the truth about yourself and the little world you create in your own image.

There is no excuse why you cannot be your own master.

5

THE FEARS YOU'LL
HAVE TO FACE

If your decision to make a change in your life were easy
and clear cut, you would have made it long ago. You would
have no difficulty looking at the facts. But it is probably
the hardest decision you will ever make and so you have
avoided making it up until now. You are unsure whether
making a change is the right thing to do. What exactly is
the right thing? Is a role right because society, friends,
relatives approve of it as the way for you to live your life?
Is a direction right just because you once made a decision
that it was right?

Look over your life and try to determine how many of
your views have changed and how many have remained
the same. You will find some very great surprises. People
do grow and change all the time. Although circumstances
and relationships may contain the same people as they did
when agreements and decisions were once made, the people who are involved in those relationships have changed,
and the agreements may not make sense in this new light.

If you do not change—that is: mature, develop new insights about yourself, alter patterns of behavior and think—

then you are very unusual indeed. People change drastically. Aging alone can do it. Sharp points mellow, angles soften, energies dwindle or new ones are discovered. A wide range of possibilities affects people. What does not happen to people is that they remain the same.

Since you do know this, it is difficult to see why you have not reevaluated old decisions made years ago in the light of incomplete knowledge and geared them to what you now know. What if your old decisions were wrong? What if you had compounded one mistake upon another, choosing things for yourself that really had more to do with how you once wanted to appear than what you were? Why should you be bound to mistakes made by a much younger you, someone whose judgment you wouldn't even consult now?

It is difficult for anyone to admit that he was wrong years ago in setting his goals. It is not clear why such mistakes should not be accepted as part of being young and inexperienced, but people resist accepting this idea.

For some people to admit that they were wrong in a choice (or that they lived a certain way because they had to) is an admission that once upon a time they were not in control of their lives, that they were powerless. This is especially difficult to admit for people who are concerned with being in a position of control.

An example is Larry, a fifty-year-old man who has lived in a shabby house with shabby furnishings for years and goes about telling people that he lives that way because it's the way he likes to live. In fact, it is not the way he likes to live at all; it's the only way he can afford to live. Instead of admitting that he would like to earn more and that he is not doing as well as he wishes, he tries to take a stand that presents him as being strong and in control of his destiny. Even when Larry inherits a small fortune, he is unable to go out and enjoy it and buy new furnishings, because that would be conceding he had been unsuccessful. He feels compelled to stay in his shabby house with the shabby furniture. It is more painful for him to give up his old notions of himself (as being powerful) than it is for him to live in a place he really doesn't like.

Larry is an example of much of what we do in our lives when we pretend to ourselves that things are going well, that we have what we want when we actually don't. It seems so difficult when things are not going our way to try to overcome them. Much of the time we fear that all we will do is uncover our own discomfort and displeasure with the way life is. We dread bumping our heads against the wall and discovering that we fear change and may be better off just dreaming, just pretending.

That is only partially true. Although everyone changes over the years, what often does not change is our fears about ourselves. After years of living we can see new strengths. Yet our attitudes toward ourselves often have not been updated; we downgrade the strengths we have developed over the years, such as self-confidence, poise or patience with others. The likelihood of finding that we are in a hopeless situation and are powerless decreases the longer we live, because our strengths tend to grow, and our ability to manage our lives increases with age. Some people get to be bigger fools as they grow older, but they are in the minority.

You climbed into the rat race to avoid something else. What you were trying to avoid was failure, insecurity and self-confrontation. It's folly to pretend that you have enough success, security, and self-satisfaction just because you no longer feel as insecure or as much a failure or as exposed as you did years ago. You are really saying that staying where you are and avoiding the things you most want is making you happy. You are trying to make the rat race sound as if it had been your original goal. That is the meaning of your confusion and coverup. If you look at yourself and how you have grown, you may find to your surprise that you have as much security as you will ever really need, that you probably have a good idea of what you're like, but it's not making you happy.

What the rat race offered you as a youngster was an escape from your insecurity, your fears of facing the world alone and also facing yourself. Many of the needs that made you choose that safe direction in the first place do not exist any more. Your ability to hold a job or run a home has been proven. You have shown people that you can fulfill your role. If you fell into the rat race during the Great Depression you may have felt that it was impossible to get a job, that any job was good and that you should feel grateful for it and not complain.

Your needs in the beginning were the needs of every young person at the beginning of the quest for identity and fulfillment. Your fears were the fears of being rejected, of being worthless as a businessman, as a mother or whatever. If you look you will see that somehow during the years many of these feelings have been mellowed by age, even if they haven't gone away. Sure, maybe you aren't the wonderchild who was going to tear the world apart—but you didn't do so badly either. Really you didn't. In the old days you were afraid you couldn't survive. The point is: why stay on at what you are doing just because you are trying to prove you can survive? You've already done that. It's time to do something else. You've grown up and your decisions about yourself have to grow up, too.

You've survived. Maybe now it's time to live.

It should be obvious when you decide to change that the people around you, who are in the same boat as you, are going to be enormously threatened by your move. More than likely they have not reevaluated themselves, and so they regard your leaving the old ways as a dire threat. Perhaps they fear that they, too, have been doing the wrong thing all their lives. You must be stopped before you upset their lives.

Your compatriots are going to be jealous. Don't expect any of them, except the most open of them, to express feelings of warmth toward you. They have to put you down because what you are doing is something they may not even be able to think of. Most likely they will agree that things could be better. Since they are not doing any better themselves, the idea of a change is something they don't really want to cope with. If you were merely talking about a change of homes or a job in a different company, it would be a different story. It would be less of a threat to others, though still upsetting. To make a real change, to give up something and start fresh somewhere, is thought to be the idea of a dreamer, a kook. In a flash you will hear all of the arguments you have been struggling with, and they'll be presented to you as if they are absolutes pointing only in one direction, the one opposite your choice.

Whether your change involves your family, your job, or just your attitude toward work, pleasure and what you consider to be important to you in life, the people you will speak to will react with fear and offer you very little comfort. What you will hear is a recitation of the reasons and rationalizations they use to keep their own minds in place. This is a very tiresome business.

Why can't they let you go? The answer is simple. Society fears a free man. Whenever society sees someone who is truly free, it feels compelled to bind him up again. The person must be branded as an outcast and categorized as odd and unconforming. Society must do this merely because, by definition, society is an arrangement of rules to be conformed to. Not to conform is not to belong in society. But you'll do well to remember: the greatest accomplishments do not necessarily happen within the confines of the usual social restrictions.

For decades artists have had the reputation of being Bohemian, with little regard for the external trappings and moral confines of society. Their lives are centered on creating. Restraints were seen as inhibiting the creative process and were removed. The rigid structure of our own society makes it increasingly difficult to be free in exercising powers of expression and creativity. The industrial society permits creativity to exist reluctantly and only because it needs the creations to increase the output of industry. The pressures of our world have become so great that most creativity can exist only outside society.

A person who is truly free to follow the dictates of his own conscience and heart threatens that part of society that depends on reliable productivity and consumption. If a person had the right to choose whether he will or will not serve in the army, stay at a boring job because he is told he is supposed to, drive a dozen screaming Cub Scouts to the zoo, then the entire distribution of labor may be upset.

When people leave the rat race, they become more whole and less of a cog in some giant apparatus of gears grinding ceaselessly toward a goal that the individual worker doesn't see or understand. Once someone is free, it becomes increasingly difficult to find meaning in attaching the same bolt to a thousand different cars every day, or to sweep the same floors each morning. The person who breaks away and becomes free, feels whole and wants to see the entire operation from beginning to end. He wants to be in control himself. He wants to feel that his entire world is his. It is a feeling of self-sustenance, increased self-worth and self-assuredness. It is the ability to say "no" to nonsense. It is being free.

To restore human dignity is difficult in our culture. It requires one to come to terms with the idea that no matter how important you are, how much you are paid, how famous you are, the only standard you can use for measuring success is whether or not what you are doing is something that comes from the part of you which you consider most important, whatever you secretly believe about yourself, your real identity. Another way of putting it is that if you were free and then given every opportunity to change, the only change should be to do more of what you are now doing. The questions remain: will the person they talk about at your funeral really be you, the special you? Or will fears shackle the special you forever?

When you decide to make a change, your spouse is going to be threatened as nothing before in your marriage has threatened her or him. To make a decision you have had to admit that you have changed and grown and in what specific ways. This admission presents your spouse with the terrifying question: has he or she outgrown me? Perhaps you no longer feel you need to be praised by your spouse for every little thing you do because you now feel sure about yourself when previously you didn't. If your spouse's role was to bolster your fallen ego, what will your spouse do now that your need for that role has changed? Perhaps your drive to accumulate material things no longer exists. Maybe you want a simpler life.

Maybe you want help in finding yourself. Well, whenever a spouse enters psychotherapy, it is common for the other spouse to become anxious and threatened by what they imagine to be going on behind their back. Often people worry that their marriage secrets will be revealed to the psychiatrist, that they are going to be "told on." In many cases this is so, but that is rarely what is really bothering these people.

The real threat of a spouse entering psychotherapy is either that a change will take place in the other that will allow him to stand on his own two feet or that changes will force the spouse who is not in therapy also to make changes. Often when a patient discovers something about his interaction in the marriage and can admit his own blame, the spouse's contribution to the difficulties at home will also no longer be overlooked. Just by being in therapy a spouse makes the demand on the other to change also. The same can be said for a spouse getting involved in encounter groups, sensitivity training, or even Women's Lib.

It is not uncommon to see a frustrated, angry husband drag his unwilling wife to a psychiatrist and demand that the psychiatrist set her straight. Bewildered, the poor woman tells her story. When she finds that she is not entirely to blame, that she has rights of her own and is entitled to make her own decisions about her life, the husband begins to denigrate the psychiatrist. The husband now has more than he bargained for. The psychiatrist cannot change his wife for him. If anything, the husband feels she is now worse. Now he needs help. Moral: don't push anyone into therapy unless you are prepared to go yourself. The head you straighten out may be your own.

To a partner who has not taken a good look at his life, your announcement that your life style may change is a great threat. It forces the other to look at his life whether or not he wants to. It was frightening enough for you to do this. Why should it be less so for him? It will even be more difficult because he is not likely to muster the same motivation that sparked you on and gave you courage to look when you were afraid. The only thing to spur him on is often the fear that if he does not change with you, he will lose you.

The fear of losing a spouse because of being outgrown is one that crosses the minds of almost everyone. Because it is so frightening, most people don't consider it for very long. This inattention is a poor idea. If you are going to outgrow your spouse (or be outgrown), pretending you are not will not change the imbalance.

Couples sometimes play interesting games when there is a change in the offing. They may use their newfound strength as a weapon to point out how ill-suited they really are for each other. Some couples who have problems in communicating may use such a drastic change as a way of forcing a separation rather than talking.

The main issue may not be dissatisfaction with the life style, but with the partner. Rather than deal with this in a straightforward way, the accused partner is made to feel as if he or she is holding the other back from fulfilling his life's work and a separation follows.

The party who has forced a split by trumping up a false issue of life style may begin that new life when in fact the new way may be less pleasing. Because it was the wedge toward the separation, it is maintained for appearances. As a result, the spouse who left is still badly off and in need of another major change, this time in life style rather than spouse. The pattern is not unlike that of a youngster entering the rat race for the first time, making a choice out of fear but convincing himself it was out of preference.

Announcing the new plans to the spouse is the same as announcing a challenge, a challenge that implies: are you up to what I want to do? Are you good enough to change, too?

The position of the man in our society makes him the one who is most apt to change. He is most likely to move ahead in the world and therefore more likely to outgrow the other. The role in which wives have been cast by many husbands is an unfair one that does not allow women to grow or develop the flexibility to adapt. In part this happens because many husbands cast wives in the part of a protective buffer whose dependable inertia serves to keep husbands from looking at themselves realistically over the years. When the husband finally decides he can look at himself and wants to change, the wife panics!

It is a tremendously difficult and stressful move. The wife has not previously been allowed the luxury of even considering changing her life. She has been made the guardian of her husband's ego by existing in a pattern that prevents threats from disturbing their life together. She is now asked to give up her role. What if she doesn't want to change? What about her vulnerability in the face of unpleasant personal insights? Suddenly she is asked to remove everything she needed to make herself comfortable over the years, and with no promise that she'll be happier in return. All she knows is that her husband wants to change. To accommodate that change she may have to give up the substitutes for her own fulfillment, perhaps the house, the comfortable ways and familiar friends that made her happy when her husband was trying to find himself. What assurances does she have that he really knows what he wants this time? Why should she take a look at herself all over again, especially if she is not promised the opportunity to fulfill herself or to follow whatever she discovers in reexamining herself? Why should it only be the husband's game?

To suggest that you are going to change, then, obviously opens the possibility that others may change as a result. Husband and wife must both consider the possibility that they have outgrown each other in some very important ways, ways that were not considered before because they were not allowed to be considered.

The other spouse may refuse to change their way of life and insist that the status quo be kept. She may say she is very content with the original arrangement made many years ago and expects its terms to be honored. This position is not an unfamiliar one, even if it is rather rigid. It represents an attempt to deny what has happened and to hide from reality.

People who adopt this attitude are the very ones who struggle to entrench the spouse in the marriage by investing the family treasure in material possessions or complex routines. Any change in life style becomes a crucial issue for such people.

When you announce your plans to a person as rigid as this you'd better be prepared to carry them through on your own. If they can defeat your plans, they will go to extremes to make sure that their interests are protected so that the subject will not come up again; or if it does, that next time they will hold all the cards. They see the desire to change as betrayal and will suspect everything you do in the future as disloyal.

Many people whom you would not have expected to react that way will be threatened by your move. Everyone has reasons why he is unable to alter or even face some unpleasant things. They feel it's okay to complain a little about the system as long as you don't disrupt it.

When a friend announces to another that he is giving up his tedious way of life (they probably share many of the same contractual things in common) he is, in a sense, saying that the friend's way of life is not optimal either. The friend listens to the problem that is unfolded to him with new insight and to the points supporting the decision, all delivered with fervor and conviction. Suddenly, the friend feels as if he is under attack, as if his beliefs are being questioned. He is not prepared to make a similar decision or even consider it.

One reason for announcing change is to drum up support—even to convince the other to consider the same move. It's the old "safety in numbers" gambit. And other people see through it and feel threatened by it.

Suppose you have decided to leave your husband and begin to list all your reasons to your best friend. More likely than not, at least half of your reasons are applicable to her own marriage. It's not uncommon to find that you and your friend have mutual difficulties, but this may just make your friend extra anxious and angry at you. Sharing your feelings about your husband and applying them to hers will often result in her trying to make you accept her rationalizations for staying together and she may begin to apply them to your own marriage.

Our society does not like us to be truly free because too much of its material success depends on our being part of the system. The system is everywhere. It is not an organized system controlled at the top, as many activists believe. Rather, it is controlled just above the middle.

The clothing industry offers a good example. We are bombarded with hundreds of exposures to fashion changes through the media. They are relatively sympathetic to giving air and page space to fashion features because the media depend on a continuing flow of advertising money from stores that sell the goods. A broad plan of indoctrination results, operating entirely independently of the government. When the youth of America decided that dressing in nice clothes is not as comfortable as wearing dungarees and old army jackets, the clothing industry faced a difficult situation; many of the fine specialty shops that cater to younger people suffered greatly. The attempt to link sloppy dress with un-American ideologies and activities seemed to find some popular support. The economic pressure brought by casual dressers encourages society to categorize their taste as part of a general antisocial attitude.

The same thing can be said for almost any other product

if one looks hard enough. Society has a method of exerting pressure to conform.

People who want to get back to simpler, self-contained ways of life are regarded as a threat to the very existence of our culture. Any country whose ideals and structure would suffer if people became free and found themselves does not meet the needs of its people, does not allow for human nature. We do need the mutual cooperation of many people to survive, but to survive with no hope for fulfilling one's dreams is to live without hope, never to be really alive.

So when you decide you want to give up on an empty struggle and find a way to make you happy because it's you, don't expect encouragement. Expect a raw trembling fear, sometimes covered with bristling anger, sometimes punctuated by a sigh of jealousy, and you will not be disappointed.

From society expect nothing. It will do what it can to undermine you. There will always be rednecks waiting to see you fall flat on your face. You may find some people who will help, mostly people who have already changed and know the way and also the people who have always wanted to break away, who have not yet found the courage but would gain great strength from your success. When society suckled you, it suckled you on the milk of interdependence, the milk of compromise. When it weaned you, it did so only after you were too bloated, too groggy with the surfeit of being taken care of. You got used to that over the years. You learned to accept it as good, to see independence as uncertainty. Interdependence became your goal because it was taught to be your goal. But you are your goals and only you can free yourself.

6

TALKING IT OVER: CONVERSATIONS WITH PEOPLE WE KNOW AND LOVE

So in spite of all you know about the way people and society feel about someone who wants to break away and be what he wants to be, you're still determined to talk over your ideas with the people you think can help you most. Well, it's no use trying to tell you what it would be like. You just have to be there.

FIRST EPISODE

Interior Day—Kitchen

It is the modern, expensive kitchen of Harriet and Stanley. Everything is highly polished and gleaming, revealing Harriet's efficiency. She is setting the table in the kitchenette for two places. The door opens and Stanley walks in. He walks over to Harriet and gives her a kiss on the neck.

HARRIET (pulling away): You're late.

(He looks annoyed.)

STANLEY: It was the traffic, besides . . .

HARRIET: . . . Besides you've had a drink or two.

(He nods and walks over to a cupboard, pulls out a bottle and proceeds to mix himself a drink. He smiles.)

STANLEY: You want one?

(She shakes her head.)

HARRIET: I have cold cuts and some chicken from last night. I didn't have time to make anything special.

STANLEY: It doesn't matter.

(He looks excited.)

HARRIET (nodding): What does any more?

(The camera moves in on STANLEY and we see him in extreme close-up. He looks concerned and in earnest.)

STANLEY (seriously): I want to talk to you.

HARRIET: No one's stopping you.

(She continues to be busy with dishes, etc.)

STANLEY: I've been doing a lot of thinking lately.

HARRIET: Go on, go on.

(She continues to work and does not look at him.)

STANLEY: You know how well those last few paintings I did went?

(She busies herself.)

HARRIET: The one of the barn that wasn't really a barn and the still life I didn't like. I'm sorry. I just don't like pictures of dead fish.

STANLEY: Well, I sold them both.

HARRIET: Sold them? (looks up at him) For how much?

STANLEY (irritated): It's not important.

HARRIET: How much?

STANLEY: Fifty dollars.

HARRIET: Each?

STANLEY (exasperated): No, for both.

HARRIET (disappointed): Oh!

STANLEY: That's not the point. The point is that I can't stand going into that brokerage office any more. I hate it.

HARRIET: Are we going through that again?

STANLEY: This time it's different. This time I feel I'm getting good at my painting. I want to get out and paint all the time. I want to quit work and spend my time painting.

HARRIET: What have you been drinking?

STANLEY (throws up his hands): It's not that. I decided the way we live is all wrong, our values, the things we're working for. (points to the opulent kitchen) All this.

HARRIET (sitting down): What are you talking about? It's a beautiful kitchen! I went two years without a fur coat for this kitchen.

STANLEY: I've decided to change things. I want to pack up and move all of us up to Maine.

HARRIET: You've decided that everything's all wrong? I suppose I am, too!

(She gets up, looks tearful.)

STANLEY: No, no, you're just fine.

HARRIET: I'm glad to hear that! What do you want for supper?

STANLEY: Can't you be serious for a minute? Can't you listen to me? Don't I rate a little attention around here?

HARRIET: When you talk crazy things like that, I don't want to listen to you.

STANLEY: I want to paint!

HARRIET: So go paint! If you want to paint, you can paint without quitting your job.

STANLEY: That's not it. I want to spend time in my own studio even if I only sell to decorators. I really love painting! I want to have my own studio, make my own hours, do what I want. I have enough savings for the moment. I've earned the right.

HARRIET: You'd be sick of it in a week. I know you. I've heard this routine before. Look at it this way: who do you think is going to buy these paintings? *I* certainly wouldn't spend twenty-five dollars on a picture of a dead fish. And the time it took to do that! You must have spent five dollars on the canvas and paint alone. It's not worth it. What kind of a living is that?

STANLEY: I want to go where I can feel whole again and in charge of things.

HARRIET: You mean all these years you've been miserable? You expect me to believe that? What's really bothering you? Why all of a sudden do you get these ideas out of thin air? A little hobby is one thing, but this is ridiculous! (as if possessed by a revelation) I know what the problem is! You need a vacation! That's not a bad idea. We both could use a vacation.

STANLEY (getting angry): Damn it, I want to become a full time artist. I know I'm not great, but we can get by. I can teach. I've taken enough lessons over the years. I want to move up to the artists' colony at Ogunquit and make a new start.

HARRIET: And just what am I supposed to do in Ogunquit during the winter? I have a life too, you know. You aren't the only one living in this house. You've got children. What about thinking of them?

STANLEY: I've thought about them. First of all, they're older and they're in school. It won't matter. They'll adjust. You'll adjust.

HARRIET: What about all *my* friends?

STANLEY: You'll make new ones. You'll find something to do.

HARRIET: I'll go crazy is what I'll do! There's nothing for me there. What am I going to do with all that time, sit and watch you paint dead fish? Is that why you want to move to Ogunquit, so you can have plenty of fish?

(She makes an attempt at a laugh. He's irritated.)

STANLEY: Look, I'm not kidding. I've been thinking about doing this for years, just a place for the two of us.

HARRIET: You can make it for the one of you. I'm not going. I think it's crazy . . . I'll adjust, hah! I don't need that kind of aggravation after all these years. You're doing just fine where you are. We have what we want, everything flows smoothly. Why would you want to spoil it?

STANLEY: It just isn't right the way it is. I don't feel right about it.

HARRIET: You will in time. I'll call the travel agent tomorrow. What about Spain?

STANLEY: I don't want to go to Spain!

HARRIET: Then maybe you'll have something to eat. We'll talk about this foolishness later.

STANLEY: This time I'm serious and this time you're going to listen!

HARRIET: Maybe you could listen, too. Maybe you're not the only one in this house who has rights. I have rights, too, and one of my rights is to have a life I like. You're always complaining about things being so bad, well, if they are so terrible, why haven't you left already? You have a lot of growing up to do, mister. You think everyone can do everything they want all the time?

STANLEY: I don't see why I can't do what I want. I've worked hard. I've been honest. I haven't done anything wrong, and wanting to paint isn't a crime. Why can't I have a life I like?

(HARRIET gets up, starts walking around the kitchen.)

HARRIET: You made those choices years ago. Before I married you, you decided what you wanted to be. I didn't bargain on you becoming a painter.

STANLEY: You knew I painted.

HARRIET: So did Winston Churchill, but he didn't stop being a statesman.

STANLEY: I don't know how to answer you.

HARRIET: Look, I know you get under a lot of pressure at the office.

STANLEY: It's not that. I really want to get away from the life we've been leading.

HARRIET: What is it? Do you want a divorce?

STANLEY: No, you don't understand. (throws up his hands)

HARRIET: Is anyone supposed to be able to understand that?

I suppose the big question is whether there is any way a person could talk to Harriet without upsetting her. The answer is no. This couple has spent so many years together keeping their real thoughts and their feelings from each other, that to express a new idea becomes seen as a form of betrayal.

Stanley obviously has always wanted to get out and paint. Harriet knows this, but in her own way belittles what he does and thinks that his freedom to act would entrap her. Although Stanley doesn't recognize it, he relies upon Harriet to act as an obstruction to his plans each time he announces them. It is very difficult to begin a life such as Stanley imagines. Without his savings he would not be able to manage at all. He says he has decided to make the change he tells Harriet, but really he is not planning to do anything. The only thing different about his announcement this time is that the feelings to leave are more intense than last time.

Eventually this episode will pass and another just like it will follow, except that it will be more intense and may have more anger directed at Harriet. Stanley's way is definitely not the way to get Harriet's cooperation. Harriet needs a great deal of support and explanation before she can be expected to be willing to move anywhere, even to a new apartment in the same building. Stanley has lived with her long enough to know this, and his failure to be gentle and to take time to tell her reveals his secret wish that she will say no and, by keeping him where he is, protect him from possible failure. All Stanley is asking for is to be told no. If Harriet were to agree, he would probably panic or make more demands until she said no again.

EPISODE TWO

Exterior Day—Woods with Pond

It is a pleasant summer day. We are in a park following two men walking across the dusty path towards a bench. MARTY is talking to his friend ALAN. They are both in their early forties.

ALAN (sitting down on the bench): Phew, am I out of shape. Getting older.

MARTY: Both of us.

(They laugh.)

ALAN: Hey, why did you want to talk to me so urgently? Huh? I got it: you've got a broad. Right, buddy? Huh, is old Alan right?

(Alan gives Marty his elbow jokingly. Marty is not so amused.)

MARTY: It's not so simple.

ALAN: A broad? Huh? Was I right?

MARTY: Yes, I've got a girl, but . . .

ALAN (interrupting): I knew it! I knew it. You can't fool me. I've known you for . . . let's see, Jesus, twenty years. You can't fool me. Is she a great looker? Huh, has she got a friend there for your old buddy? Does she have her own apartment? That's great when a chick has her own apartment. Look, I can work it so we can bring up a bottle on my bowling night and socko, both of us in there, two broads, great!

MARTY: This is a little more complicated.

ALAN: She's not pregnant? You didn't knock the chick up? What a dumb thing to do!

MARTY: No, she's not pregnant.

ALAN: You've got the clap? Christ, and I've been touching you. Can you get VD just by touching someone?

(Wipes his hands on the bench.)

MARTY (very annoyed): Will you stop it and listen to me and let me talk? It's not like any of that. Peggy—

ALAN: Peggy. Hey, that's a cute name.

MARTY (loudly): Peggy and I have a very serious relationship.

ALAN (applauding): Great, you can keep giving it to her on the side for years.

MARTY: No, you don't understand. I met her in New York last year. She was working in a book store. I was looking for something. I don't remember. We started talking and she was just so warm and bright and interested. I stayed in the store for a couple of hours and then met her for a drink.

ALAN: And whammo!

MARTY: Nothing like it. We just talked. For five hours. It was incredible. We liked the same things. All the things I try to get Helen to do and she hates, Peggy really likes.

(ALAN looks quizzically at MARTY.)

MARTY: I found that there were a lot of things I wanted and wasn't getting at home. Things I guess I really knew about, but somehow hid from myself. And with this girl they're all right out there. I suddenly realize what I need and want.

ALAN: Look, a little strange stuff on the side never hurt anyone.

MARTY: I'm not just talking about sex. Although sex with her is great, I'm talking about finding another person who is like me. You know, even though I've known Helen since we were kids, I really feel alone when I'm with her.

I never knew what that feeling was before. I always had a restless feeling even when we were on vacation. I guess I've always wanted to be someplace else, but never found a place where I was comfortable. Then I found that what I wanted was not a place but a person.

ALAN: Hey, you've really got it bad! I mean you're really hooked on this girl. Look, everyone feels that way about their wives, Marty, that's the way life is. You can't expect your wife to be like a single girl, with all those interests. Your wife has responsibilities, your kids for instance. Don't you think other people feel frustrated all the time? Look, you're losing your perspective on this thing. I can tell just by looking at you.

(Puts his hand on MARTY's shoulder.) Hey, pal, look, she's just another girl.

MARTY (brushing his hand away): That's just the problem. She's not! Helen, my loving wife, is the one who's just another girl. I believed that Helen was different when I married her. I saw in Helen all the things I needed to see, that I wanted. You know, most of them aren't there and never were. I began to resent that over the past few years more and more and began to wonder whether I'd ever get what I wanted. But I never faced up to it. Then I met Peggy and everything I wanted was there.

ALAN: How do you know you're just not seeing things in her the way you did with Helen?

MARTY: I know me now. I know what I want. I've taken a year before I made my decision.

ALAN: Decision? What decision are you talking about? Hey, wait a minute!

MARTY: I'm going to leave Helen.

ALAN: What about your goddam kids? I mean, what

about Helen? You just can't pick up and leave. You've got a big house and a lot of responsibilities. Jesus, Marty, something's happened to you. Why can't you just have something on the side and wait till it blows over?

MARTY: I tried it. But I can't bear being away from her. When I'm with her I feel that's my life and the world makes sense for the first time.

ALAN: Christ, this sounds like it should be in the movies. This isn't real. People just don't do things like this. What would happen if everyone ran away with the first little piece who came around? You can't do it, Marty! Look at it any way you want. It just doesn't make any sense. You'll put your job in danger, you'll get your kids upset. You've always been very close to your father-in-law. Christ, look at the start he gave you two! You can't do a thing like that to him.

MARTY: I'm not doing anything to him or to anyone else. I'm doing something for me. For Marty, who decided to look at himself and be honest for the first time in his life. No one owns me. I need that girl, I love that girl. I have a lot of feeling for all these people in my life. I love my children. I even love Helen, but it's different. Helen loves me because of Helen. Peggy loves me because of me.

ALAN: You're confusing me. Helen loves you.

MARTY: Sure she loves me, because I'm her husband. She can't even risk thinking about not loving me because that would destroy her world. And she really doesn't know me. She really has her own little world. She loves me in her way, but that just doesn't seem to be enough anymore.

ALAN: I don't understand you, you've changed.

MARTY: I don't think so. I think I've always felt this way, but I was afraid to admit it to myself.

ALAN: I think you're being foolish. You're forty-three years old. You're not a kid any more. Buddy, you've got to start acting your age.

MARTY: I am acting my age for the first time in my life. I'm looking at who I am and what I need and what I want out of life. And I need her.

ALAN: You sound like the lyrics of some pop song.

MARTY: You know, that's funny. I never listened to them before. Some of them make sense to me now.

ALAN: This is all very unrealistic. I'm surprised at you. I mean, letting a situation like this get the best of you. The problem is you just aren't handling this right.

MARTY: I can't handle it any other way.

ALAN: Look. You've got a girl. That doesn't mean you have to go messing up your entire life. That's silly and very expensive. You just have to keep things going smoothly.

MARTY: No, I'm going to leave Helen.

ALAN: Hey, don't you think you should talk this over with someone?

MARTY: Who? What for? To get permission? I'm a big boy. I know what I want. I know what I want for the first time.

ALAN: Well, I'd be failing in my duties as a friend if I didn't tell you that I think you're crazy, that you're acting impulsively, that you're going to regret it. And I think it's a pretty shitty thing to do to all these people.

MARTY: Would I be doing Helen a favor by staying with her if I didn't love her? Don't you think she deserves to spend her life with someone who really loves her?

ALAN: I don't know what to say. Carole and I have our problems. Everyone does. I don't expect miracles or for her to be some kind of fantastic sex pot, and I manage to keep things in line. Yuh, I admit she doesn't always understand, but who understands everyone all the time? I wouldn't bust up my marriage because of that.

MARTY: No one is asking you to.

ALAN: You should wait a while. You'll probably get over it. I'd wait.

Why did Marty even bother to talk over things with Alan? Clearly, he should know that Alan seems to represent the forces of inertia and would resist any sort of change. Alan is not especially concerned about the morality of the situation; in fact, he has much less resistance about having an affair than Marty. Alan is upset because an institution is about to be threatened. Alan is more concerned with the preservation of a marriage for its own sake than for the feelings of the partners involved.

In fact, Alan's projections are so stereotyped that it is almost unnecessary for Marty to refute them. Marty can go on thinking that Alan is a narrow-minded person who could not understand such things, a hypocrite who could fool around with a hundred women and, as long as he stayed married, would believe he was doing the best thing. By comparison with Alan, Marty can feel some measure of moral superiority. The home, the children and other responsibilities are still important to Marty. He managed to get Alan to justify them as the reasons for staying in a marriage, which he doesn't agree with and which, coming from Alan, appear less threatening, easier to refute, even though Marty knows they are in part true.

Marty wishes to act on the basis of feelings he has thought about for a year and about which he is still not entirely sure. What he has done is to use Alan, an eager spokesman for the establishment, to give a predictable response.

He gets Alan to express his feelings about many things, among which are the issues Marty is still hesitant about. Because Marty disagrees with so much of what Alan says, he finds it easy to group all of Alan's objections together and to reject them. Somehow he now feels freer to move, that only people like Alan get upset over these painful issues. Marty has not dealt with all his concerns and uses Alan's negativism to help justify leaving.

What Marty was asking for was a way of feeling better about making his decision. There are some aspects of any decision that one cannot feel good about. To try to get others to help justify your actions will not alleviate these doubts and may create enemies. In the end you must deal with all the feelings and issues of every move yourself.

EPISODE THREE

Interior Day—Sitting Room

It is a well-appointed sitting room decorated in large overstuffed chairs and flowered drapes with Currier and Ives prints. It is the home of FRAN, an attractive woman of about thirty-five, talking to her MOTHER.

MOTHER: Well, why all the secretiveness? Why did you want me to come over?

FRAN: I have something very difficult to decide, and I really need your help.

MOTHER: Go ahead, I'll try.

FRAN: This is going to sound awful, but you're the only one I can talk to, really.

MOTHER: Go ahead, dear.

FRAN: I'm not completely sure, but I think I want to leave Tom.

MOTHER (practically shouting): What? What are you talking about?

FRAN: I'm not really happy here.

MOTHER: What do you mean? (pointing): Look at this house and all the other things you have! That man would give you absolutely everything you asked for! You have more than I ever did, I can tell you that. I had to push your father for everything I got.

FRAN: Maybe what I've got isn't what I want.

MOTHER: You certainly wanted it when you married him.

FRAN: Maybe I just thought I did.

MOTHER: Oh, come on now, you can argue that way about everything if you want. I may be old, but I'm no fool. Young lady, if you hadn't grabbed Tom, someone else would've. He's been everything to you.

FRAN: That's right, Mother, but I was twenty when I got married, and it was easy for him to be everything to me. I didn't know what I wanted.

MOTHER: Sounds like you still don't, if you ask me.

(MOTHER pours a drink for herself.)

FRAN: He's good to me. I mean he loves me, and he works hard. But somehow the way he loves me doesn't do anything for me. It doesn't make me feel special or good inside.

MOTHER: Well, after having three kids is one hell of a time to discover that.

FRAN: I don't know. I guess I love him, but kind of the same way I love you. I don't feel inside like I do with . . .

MOTHER (shocked and abruptly): With whom?

FRAN: A man I've been seeing.

MOTHER: Who? What's his name?

FRAN: It doesn't matter.

MOTHER: What do you mean it doesn't matter?

FRAN: It matters, but you don't need to know yet.

MOTHER: Yet. What do you mean yet?

FRAN: Oh, it's such a long story. I met him two years ago and it progressed from friendship into a beautiful relationship.

MOTHER: You're not sleeping with him, are you?

FRAN (confused by MOTHER's not really understanding such things): I'm in love with this man, Mother.

MOTHER: Do you sleep with him?

FRAN (with a trace of belligerence): Yes, of course. I love him.

MOTHER: This is what I brought you up to be?

FRAN: Mother, it isn't like that! You're making it sound so dirty.

MOTHER: Turning your back on a wonderful husband like Tom and those three children isn't a dirty thing to do? What would you call it, an act of Christian charity?

FRAN: I've been thinking this over for a while, Mother. I really want your help. I never felt the things I feel for this man with Tom. The idea of going through life without them seems very incomplete.

MOTHER: You have everything you need to feel complete in life! What's wrong with you? What do you need to be satisfied? What did I raise? I'm just glad your father isn't here. I don't know what he'd do.

FRAN: I care for Tom a great deal, but he just isn't aware of my feelings and needs, even when I tell him. He tries very hard, but even when things are very good, they aren't special. I still feel like most of me is a stranger to him.

MOTHER: Well, don't you talk to him? You were always such a big one for talking out your problems.

FRAN: We talk, but there seems to be a limit to what he can really understand about me. No matter how hard I try to explain he doesn't understand. I'm still a mystery. He asks me if there is anything he can do. I don't think there is. He is who he is. He's very kind and very good.

MOTHER: Well it's nice to hear you say that. What about the children? Are you planning to abandon them, too?

FRAN (wincing): I've been responsible for taking care of a child ever since I was twenty-one. I never held back for one moment for my sake. It was always them first. Well, now that Bobby's turned eleven, I suddenly realized that I had time to start thinking about myself. And the thing I've come to realize is that I've done all I was expected to do in this house. I've done for everyone. I've never thought of doing for me.

MOTHER: It seems to me like Tom has given you plenty.

FRAN: It meant a lot once, but it doesn't mean as much to me now. I can walk around touching furniture when I feel lonely. Mother, I feel lonely even when Tom is around! He just exists in my life like another piece of furniture. He doesn't seem able to come into my life.

MOTHER: Well, I never thought it would happen in our family. I always thought other people were the ones whose homes broke up, not us. Do you know there has never been a divorce on my side of the family and only one on your father's, and that one was because Albert was a drunk?

FRAN: I suppose now I'm going to spoil the record? What do people in our family do when they're unhappy with each other? Do they just stick it out and live a miserable life because they don't want to ruin the record? Or is everyone in our family happy?

MOTHER: I don't like your tone of voice. Someone in your situation has no right to talk down to others. Of course people have problems, but they learn to live with them.

FRAN: Why should I be forced to live with someone I don't really love for the rest of my life?

MOTHER: You don't even know what love is. Love is not this passionate business you see in the movies. It's putting up with the day-to-day boredom, making meals, bringing up kids, trying to make a decent life for each other. What you're talking about is cheap sex and frankly, Fran, you sicken me. You really do.

FRAN: But I want more than just this. I *know* there is more than just this.

MOTHER: So become a volunteer at the hospital. Take up sewing. You don't do very much with yourself. Do something. It'll take your mind off this foolishness.

FRAN: Look, I got my degree in college and that meant nothing. I found a part-time job several times. I never felt good then either. I kept trying to substitute things for the feelings I wasn't getting. Maybe some day I'd be able to work again and enjoy it, but to try it without feeling loved seems so hopeless. It's not foolishness. It's what I never had before and what I never knew existed. It's like learning how to feel and care for the very first time. I mean, now I can look back on the way I used to feel. Getting married so young was so wrong for me. You should have objected.

MOTHER: Why? Tom was a lovely boy from a fine family, and he loved you. Maybe you think it would have been better if I'd let you run around wild for a few years like some of the kids nowadays.

FRAN: But don't you ever feel like running and being free?

MOTHER: It doesn't matter what I feel. I'm not having an affair. I'm managing my life.

FRAN: Sitting home, staying in the old routine, doing nothing but gossiping! You call that a life?

MOTHER: You have no right to talk to me like that! A lot of hard-working people spent their lives giving to you so that you could become something. You've had everything and look what you want to do with it!

You asked for advice, so I'll give you advice. I wouldn't discuss this with anyone else. It makes you look foolish and it's an insult to our family. You stay right where you are and say no to this man! In time you'll forget all about him. I know.

FRAN: Do you, Mother?

Fran has made one of the stupidest mistakes anyone can make by telling her mother about her affair. When a parent is told about his children's sexual affairs there is a strong urge to react to that child as if the child is still twelve years old. As a result, Fran put her mother in the same position of authority that she held all through Fran's youth. Fran was reduced to being a child again.

Fran may appear very wishy-washy, but not because she really is. It is because she is talking to her mother as a child confessing a crime. Fran feels guilty about what she wants to do. Part of her guilt comes from the shame of disappointing her mother and upsetting family tradition, but another part comes from being angry at mother for sitting by while she made the mistake of getting married too early in the first place.

Fran is unable to state her side of the question very clearly and, frankly, bungles it miserably. As a result, she paints a picture of herself as an empty-minded, pleasure-seeking, irresponsible woman. This is precisely what mother would have thought of anyone making such a decision, regardless of how sound the reasons behind it might be. Fran knew that because she grew up with mother. Yet that did not stop her from trying to get her mother's blessing and her mother's understanding for what she is doing.

Fran does not need this blessing or support because she is a grown woman. What she is seeking from her mother is the advice which she feels she never got before she married. So, she recreates the situation in which a girl and her mother discuss an indiscretion. It creates a great deal of anger at Fran from Mother, which allows Fran to feel punished and less guilty.

If Fran could have given her real reasons for leaving, a different picture would have emerged. Tom is not a good husband. He is a compulsive worker who comes home late every night. He refuses to take vacations. He guards all cash as if he's about to be robbed. He is happiest just napping on the sofa. He does not like to be with people. He is unaffectionate and rigid in his response to Fran's attempts to discuss anything. Tom "knows" how things should be and keeps up appearances so no one could ever suspect that he is really cold and ungiving.

111

By presenting only part of the story, Fran has both prejudiced her mother against her and made it easier for her to say that Mother was wrong.

EPISODE FOUR

Interior Day—Office

It is a psychiatrist's office. The psychiatrist is in a comfortable chair talking with a patient, a businessman in his late forties.

PATIENT: I'm having a lot of trouble falling asleep nights again.

DOCTOR (nodding): What do you think is going on?

PATIENT: Well, I know it's nothing with my wife like last time, because things are better than they've been in years.

DOCTOR: Hmmm.

PATIENT: As a matter of fact, we've been talking over some ideas I've had for some time. Ideas that I guess I thought were too silly even to talk about to you.

DOCTOR: You know that nothing is too silly to . . .

PATIENT: Yes, well, I guess this isn't so silly at all, but it sounds it.

DOCTOR (curious): Yes?

PATIENT: I've been looking at the way I live. I know I make a very good income. I have everything that is supposed to make me happy and, you know, it just doesn't seem to be what I want. You know, we got to thinking last summer when we were in Italy, you remember, I rented a car to get off the beaten path. We discovered a little inn where we were planning to stay overnight. But it turned out that the host and hostess were so warm and congenial, you know, the food so good, and the bar and whole atmosphere so congenial that we stayed for a week.

DOCTOR (nodding): I remember you telling me this.

PATIENT: But what I didn't tell you was that the place stuck in my mind. The host seemed so pleased with what he was doing and worked alongside his wife. They enjoyed making people happy. Well, I, you know, mentioned to my wife that I envied them, and she told me she'd been thinking about them, too, and also envied them.

DOCTOR: And?

PATIENT: We started to think about what it would be like to just get up and start an inn of our own—maybe ten or twelve rooms in New England somewhere. Maybe the Berkshires or in the ski country. Just a small little inn. Now we think of it all the time.

DOCTOR: A pleasing fantasy . . . What do you suppose the two of you are finding difficult to look at in your own lives?

PATIENT: Actually, there doesn't seem to be much. We get along well . . . uh . . .

DOCTOR: Perhaps the interest in opening an inn has sidetracked you from the issues of disagreement between you.

PATIENT: No . . . uh . . . not that either. You know, when I first started coming here I told you how much pressure I felt under at the job, and how much I disliked many of the things there. Talking about that has helped, but I still have stomach cramps and I still get diarrhea and feel nauseous a lot of the time. But I feel better than I did.

Is there anything wrong with leaving that job? I mean why do I have to cope with those conditions?

DOCTOR: We should ask why *do* you cope with them?

PATIENT: Because I need the money. Because I'm trained in that area. Because I spent such a long time there. I know all that.

DOCTOR: Yes, you do.

PATIENT: Maybe it's that job that's making me sick.

DOCTOR: You know better than that. People are what they are . . . a certain pattern of behavior. Your pattern is one which produces abdominal discomfort and anxiety under pressure.

PATIENT: Okay, but why do I have to be under pressure? Why can't I go somewhere where there is no pressure?

DOCTOR: Do you think that is really possible?

PATIENT: You tell me that I have trouble with authority figures. Okay, why can't I have my own establishment where I am the only authority figure?

DOCTOR: You will still feel the need to please others. That's one of the needs you have. We've talked about it at length.

PATIENT: Why do I have to change? Why can't I just do something where the need to please is an asset, where people respect and appreciate the need to please? People would appreciate someone who was an attentive innkeeper, serving drinks, waiting on bar, attending to details. You know, even though I have two secretaries I still like to do details myself.

DOCTOR: You get rid of your anxieties in small details.

PATIENT: Why can't I just change my environment?

DOCTOR: Is that really possible? Look at it. Aren't you just running away from it?

PATIENT: I don't know why I'm beating around the bush like this and just can't come out and tell you. I guess I'm afraid of rejection.

DOCTOR: The old problem with authority again!

PATIENT: Yes, yes. I know. Well, here goes. My wife and I decided to put the house up for sale, take our savings and move away. We found a lovely, enormous farmhouse near Stowe and are also considering a place near Jacob's Pillow. Once we've decided which one to take, we're going to renovate it ourselves. It'll be great fun. Painting, doing the floors, building, opening the place for business. We've even got a name.

DOCTOR: This sounds a bit impulsive.

PATIENT: I would like to pass papers next week on one of the places and move up in a few weeks. I know that isn't much time, but I want to get at it. We've never been this excited about anything before.

DOCTOR: What about your appointments?

PATIENT: Yes, I was wondering about that.

DOCTOR: You have scheduled appointments three afternoons a week.

PATIENT: Well, how do you work things like that . . . in a situation like this? I'm not going to be here.

(A long pause.)

DOCTOR: You have agreed to three appointments. When you are not here, there is no one else to fill them. What am I supposed to do with three empty hours a week? You know I have had to turn patients away because the hours were reserved for you. They are *your* hours.

PATIENT: But I'm not going to be here.

DOCTOR: You are still scheduled to be here. Don't you think that you should work this sudden change of plans through? It seems flimsily constructed, running away to some place, not even being sure where you'll be going, all this based on the wish to avoid what seems to me to be some of the crucial features of your life pattern. Features, I must remind you, which I do not think you can leave behind you. I've seen you fall down before.

PATIENT: You think I will still have problems?

DOCTOR: Maybe even worse, because if you still have problems after you've tried to escape them, then it's more difficult to pretend that the problem is outside of you. You'll have to face the problem as part of you. That can be very difficult.

PATIENT: But I know what the problem is and talking about it doesn't seem to help.

DOCTOR: You haven't given the therapy a chance to work. It takes time. You must be patient. It's unrealistic to expect something as complex as your problems to clear up overnight. After all, it took a lifetime to acquire these problems. How do you think a change like this could possibly make a permanent difference?

PATIENT: Well, I'm going to try, and after next week, I won't be coming any more.

DOCTOR: You have three appointments scheduled each week. I'll be here.

If you are seeing a psychiatrist like this, fire him and find someone who will treat you like a human being. The drive to change is precious and often short-lived if it does not find support or expression in action. To analyze all the components of any wish is impractical and impossible.

The character of the doctor is intentionally overdrawn as a caricature to illustrate how therapeutic intervention can be therapeutic interference. While psychotherapy can be immeasurably helpful in helping some people to clarify problems (which in turn allows them to change), the final decision is supposed to be the patient's, not the psychiatrist's. The great majority of people in the world make their decisions without the help of professionals in the psychological sciences. Psychiatrists themselves run the danger of thinking themselves omnipotent and omniscient, of having more impact on their patients' lives than they really do. To believe that the psychotherapeutic contribution to change is the most significant part of change is unrealistic and cannot be proven even though many people who change after seeing a psychiatrist believe it.

Psychiatrists are marvelous for telling fortunes backwards. They can predict what probably *happened* to you in your life. When it comes to telling the future, they are not much better than anyone else. If they are better, it is often because they know more about you.

Future events in a person's life are unpredictable although the style of his actions in response to those events is well understood. At best it is a matter of probabilities. We can help people understand themselves by looking at what has happened to them and teach them how to examine what they feel. Ideally, psychotherapy should allow you to see how you acted, how you feel.

When the forces toward change are present and offer the chance for fulfillment, analyzing them can be overdone. Psychiatrists are trained to be objective and to take their own bias into consideration when dealing with patients' problems. Most psychiatrists do try to be objective, but it is difficult to be objective about the cultural values with which one has grown up. Doctors struggle very hard and long to become doctors. Hard work and self-denial are part of what they have accepted in their own lives as their ideals. The psychiatrist, or anyone else for that matter, may have his own axe to grind, his own corner of the establishment to maintain, or his own bank account to keep secure. It is possible for a psychiatrist to reinforce the negative aspects of your decision. In the end you must make the decision on your own. When the drive is strong, the chances of success are best. There is nothing like feeling better to make you feel better, nor anything like success to help you succeed.

EPISODE FIVE

Interior Day—Rectory Office

It is the office of a MINISTER sitting with a lady parishioner. He is going through his mail.

MINISTER: I'm so glad you could come at this hour. I know it's inconvenient, but my schedule . . .

(Writing on a small piece of paper.)

LADY: Oh no, I understand. Thank you.

MINISTER: Well, how can I help you?

(Reads a leaflet.)

LADY: I really didn't want to come, but John, my husband, insisted that someone talk to me. He thinks I'm foolish.

MINISTER: Well, you know husbands. What did he mean, do you suppose?

(Lights pipe.)

LADY: I told him I wanted to open a dress shop of my own. I'm very good with my hands.

MINISTER: And what did he say?

LADY: He said my place was in the home with the children.

MINISTER: And you disagreed?

LADY: No. I agreed, but I also want a part of my life that's my own, something private.

MINISTER (conspiratorially): You feel you have something to hide?

LADY: No. What should I have to hide?

MINISTER: Why isn't your home satisfying to you? (Relaxing, puffing the pipe.)

LADY: It is, but only in some ways. I need more.

MINISTER: The trouble with people today is that they always feel they need more. I think that the emotional and spiritual values get lost in this ever increasing greed for more. I don't mean to insinuate that you are self-indulgent.

LADY: All I want is to take some time in the mornings when the children are at school and make dresses to order and have a shop to call my own. I don't want more money. I just want something I can call my own.

MINISTER: Well, that would be nice if it worked, but not everything we plan works out the way we wanted it to. Your husband understands that. He knows his role as the head of the household, and, frankly, I may speak quite frankly with you, may I?

(She nods.)

I think your husband finds the idea of your working upsetting. Perhaps his male ego or something like that. Your working would make it hard for him to function. He cannot transcend his identity. I've spoken with him about that.

LADY: Oh, I see.

(She doesn't.)

MINISTER (as if concluding a sermon): You know, sometimes we give up a lot of the things we want for higher goals. The concept of sacrifice is one which has been too much neglected in our modern lives, and I think you would do well to consider it.

LADY: But, why must *I* be the one to sacrifice?

MINISTER: Perhaps it's better not to question the reasons behind giving. There is sometimes a meaning which is not always ours to understand. I do hope you'll excuse me, but I do have another appointment. I hope we've straightened something out for you. If you'd like to talk about it next week or the week after . . .

Actually, it's the husband who has the problem in this situation. His poor wife is not being taken seriously by anyone. The difficulty she is running into with her minister is that he just isn't understanding her. While many of the clergy have excellent backgrounds in pastoral counseling, it becomes difficult for some of them to put aside the male point of view and, more particularly, the religious connotations they see around them. Often, they find religious meanings in matters that are not primarily religious. This is the natural leaning of a person who has chosen such a life, but it may have little to add to the solution of a problem. It just compounds the guilt.

To imply that the misery on this earth and the misery in the lives and occupations of individuals is justifiable on religious grounds is to make a perversion of the religion one pretends to interpret. In the Middle Ages, people were told that their silent acceptance of their miserable lot was the way God meant it to be, that their sacrifice was a noble thing. The upper castes preached the same line to the untouchables. It is a natural tendency of man to try to preserve what he believes is his way of life and to protect it from outside threats.

Any institutionalized way of thinking eventually must reject the individual who threatens its structure. The obvious conclusion is drawn at the first sign of heresy: what if everyone else followed the example?

The moral: only go to the people in the long established institutions for guidance when you want to be told to stay where you are. Some exceptions exist, but they are rare and often are the opinions of people who are themselves about to break with the traditions of their institution, who themselves are soon to be called outcasts.

EPISODE SIX

Interior Day—Office

It is a large, well outfitted private top executive's office. The BOSS and CHARLIE have been talking for some moments. The BOSS appears puzzled and agitated.

BOSS: Can we run this all down from the top again? I must be getting old or something.

CHARLIE: I've decided to quit work, sell the house and take a place in the country and write.

BOSS: Charlie, you're the best lawyer in Los Angeles! You want more money? I'll speak to Judd Clarke and we'll see what we can do.

CHARLIE: No, I don't want more money.

BOSS: Charlie, are you negotiating with me? Come on, I'm your friend! You can be straight with me.

CHARLIE: I *am* being straight with you. I just want to leave and do what I want.

BOSS: You don't like it here!

(Puts his arm around CHARLIE.)

CHARLIE: Max, you're a prince! A real prince. I wouldn't want a better boss than you. But why have a boss at all?

BOSS: Charlie, Charlie, you don't make any sense. Sixty-five thousand bucks a year! That's enough to support even your wife . . .

Oho! You got something on the side that you need more money for?

CHARLIE: No. I just want to write.

BOSS: Am I hearing things today? Why on earth would a guy like you—what are you, forty, forty-five?

CHARLIE (hurt): Thirty-nine. Has this place aged me that much?

BOSS: Responsibility makes people look older. You've got a responsible position. You're young. Why would a guy like you want to give all this up?

CHARLIE: I want to write.

BOSS: Charlie, a word of advice. Don't do it, Charlie . . . you'll regret it. You know what I mean. I can see letting someone have a little extra time, but you can't keep me hanging on like indefinitely. I'd have to find someone else. I mean, Charlie, you're good, but I'll find someone who can do your work just as well. I mean you're not irreplaceable here, Charlie. So be straight with me.

CHARLIE: I am being straight. I'm leaving.

BOSS: But why?

CHARLIE: Maybe to find something that only I can do, that's irreplaceable.

BOSS: You're not making sense, Charlie.

From everything we have seen, it should be possible to construct some guidelines about talking to people about plans as radical as these. First of all, because plans are likely to appear impulsive to most people, you should have a good idea about what you really want and be fairly sure about them before you begin to talk to anyone. You should never speak to someone who is incapable of offering anything but a negative response because of his own point of view. One should never approach a person who has the same kind of problems and is unwilling to look at them. They are only able to steer you away from their problems at best. At worst, they become projective and destructive, playing out their own inadequacies on you.

Don't go around telling everyone you meet about everything you plan to do. You may have become very excited and pleased with yourself, but remember that people are not used to seeing someone become free and fulfill himself. It frightens them, and the only way that they can deal with you is to categorize you as having gone off the deep end. Other people's views and opinions are dependent more on their feelings than on the facts and you should not let other people influence your decisions too much. It is not necessary to alienate people just because you have a big mouth.

When separation or divorce is the issue, keeping your

mouth shut as long as possible is the best bet by far, even going as far as to deny what is going on to everyone except a very few chosen intimates. Rumors may start and rumors get out of control. While settlements and legal contests may promise to go smoothly, a rumor at the wrong time can disrupt everything.

Discussing changes with older people is dangerous. Parents and friends who have clearly made many compromises and have not had the nerve to break out on their own will only react with great anxiety. They must deny what you say or get very angry at you. It is a surefire reaction, and it is doubtful that you will get anything out of it besides being yelled at. Unless this is one of your hidden motives (getting other people to punish you for doing something you feel is wrong), then it's pretty useless. It's even useless if you do want to get yelled at. Leave the old timers alone!

Some people have a large investment in maintaining the status quo. Many members of the clergy are committed to reinstate spiritual values even when these are not in the picture. Spiritual values are important, but they are frequently different from emotional needs. When commitments have been colored with religious overtones, they tend to be viewed as less subject to change than otherwise. This is a stumbling block that is finally beginning to be moved as people realize it's man who makes and interprets the rules and it's one's own conscience that must rule in the end.

Doctors are more institutional-establishment oriented than most people and often have remarkably little flexibility in viewing change. If they can be forgiven for this, it's because no one in our society has as much invested in time and effort in what they are. Doctors tend to see people who do not struggle and conquer as weaker. Psychiatrists are less rigid and tend to be more lenient, but they are also human. Even though many would disagree with the comment that follows, they know it is often true. Psychiatrists often have difficulty letting patients go out on their own when the patient feels the urge. The psychiatrist is often committed to understand everything that is going on and is afraid to act in the face of incomplete evidence. Also, the structure of his work week is such that the loss of a patient is a financial difficulty. So a patient may be encouraged to stay on in part for the doctor's sake.

By the same token, one should not talk to people who can only give you the positive side of a situation. The best people to speak with are people you can trust, who really wish the best for you and have enough insight into their own lives to know that they can have faults, too. Your doing something about your problems then cannot mean that they are also threatened to act and will have to reject you.

People who have been through similar difficulties are also very helpful, but they are not always easy to find. And they have the peculiar difficulty of wanting others to do the same thing just so they can see another number added to their side. Safety in numbers again. If enough people do it, they reason, it must be right. One can feel pressured by these people if you have not yet come to terms with your own wishes before you speak to them.

It's important to know the question you want answered before you speak to someone. If you can't form the question, you've got some thinking to do. The big question, "Am I doing the right thing?" is a question only you can answer. What seems right to others may have little relationship to what you need or do. If you merely wish to share what you feel with someone else, you should question whether you really want approval and then use the above guide.

The real question is: what is your life worth and what are you going to do with it? When you talk this over with others you merely bring out their hostility and their own guilt.

7
WHERE GUILTS COME FROM

Even if you feel like starting over right now, you probably couldn't. You couldn't stand up and say, "I already gave, enough is enough." You might *want* to say it. In fact, you might want to say it this minute, but you can't because you'd still feel guilty about it.

The very first step and probably the most important in managing guilt is to understand it. Before discussing the way guilt holds people back, it is useful to know how guilt works.

When a person suffers a real or imagined loss he feels hurt. Because something has been taken away, he feels empty or worthless. As a result, he becomes angry at the person he believes hurt him. If his anger is not resolved or allowed to be expressed, it will grow and lead to feelings of guilt. Guilt is anger that has turned inward. If unchecked, it may lead to feelings of depression. Anxiety is the fear of the loss in the first place. This also may be real or imagined.

People often feel guilty when they shift their roles from sacrificing for others to fulfilling themselves. The sacrificing person, even though he may not like it, fulfills his obligations and does his duty. Somehow, even though his life may be unpleasant, he can live with himself. The unpleasantness is accepted as a form of punishment.

People who feel guilty generally feel better when they are punished from the outside because there is less need for them to punish themselves. Some people do get into situations that are painful to endure and stay there for a long time. As much as they complain about the "unfairness" and the punishment they take, they feel better. The pain allows them to spend their energies in ways other than punishing themselves. Of course, this can be overdone and the punishment can be made so difficult that the guilt-carrier becomes downtrodden and accomplishes little.

I knew an executive who tolerated long hours, a demanding boss and poor pay for many years. He complained bitterly to everyone who would listen. He was so exhausted by the piles of work he brought home at nights and on weekends that he was a stranger to his family and was unable to relate to anything but his job. Throughout much of his life he felt guilty about the death of his mother when he was eight. His anger at the mother was almost unendurable for him and he found it difficult to cope with. He recalled feelings, first as a child and later as an adolescent, of being worthless and bad because he was so angry most of the time. The only time he felt comfortable was when he was overworked and directed his anger at his boss. Just after his son's eighth birthday his guilt began to return, and in order to feel better he buried himself in work. In psychotherapy he realized that he was envious of his son for having a mother when, at the same age, he did not. And he was able to understand his anger and resolve it. He was able to allow himself time with his family and even to pursue a hobby. He did not change his job, but he did begin to manage it differently and delegated work to others for the first time. He no longer felt that he had to shoulder all the burdens around him.

Sometimes people take unappealing positions and continue in unpleasant careers as if trying to prove that they are self-denying. It is as if they allow their disagreeable lives to bear witness for them, to show that they are decent people.

We have already discussed some of the possible motivations behind career choices. In addition, a career may be a means of mastering threatening feelings. For example, prison guards are sometimes attracted to their jobs (where they help to control inmates' dangerous impulses) because the guards may fear their own impulses. Some people become involved in charity to balance feelings of greed that they feel guilty about.

A career choice that helps control one's own feelings is difficult to change; to give it up would be like losing the psychological security it offers. Characteristically, when people in such a situation do change, they find another one that offers the same sort of controls. It seems that if you need help to manage your feelings, you will find it and pay dearly for it.

So, while a particular career or situation may appear very unpleasant to a casual observer, it is that very unpleasantness that makes the person feel better. When you feel guilty, you try to get someone to punish you. If you can't find anyone, you will probably end up doing the job yourself, and you will usually be much harder on yourself than anyone else. Until these underlying feelings are discovered and dealt with, you remain at their mercy.

There is no need to spend your life tied to a wheel. Professional help is often very useful in breaking through this seemingly unending cycle of guilt.

Many other sources of guilt keep upsetting our lives. I have already mentioned some of the conflicts between young people and their parents. Now let's take a look at some of the effects of these conflicts. Many of the choices that adolescents make are a reaction against the parents as much as they are intended to satisfy the young person's own life needs. A major need of the adolescent is to be able to do what he wants to shape his own self. Adolescents often feel they must exercise their freedom by choosing the exact opposite of what their parents want, even if they agree with them. It is angry and self-defeating behavior leaving scars that are a long time in healing. In fact, many of the rigid attitudes that are so difficult to vacate later in life originate when young people strike out on their own in a spiteful way.

Let's examine a situation of an adolescent conflict resulting in an impulsive and incompatible marriage.

Guilt finds many ways to get transformed into a way of life during adolescence. Some girls are frightened over the prospect of having sexual relations or live in dread of losing control of their emotions and doing something objectionable to their parents. The parents may convey their fear to the daughter: that she will become sexually promiscuous and bring shame upon the house. The daughter is struck by two major realizations. First, that her parents do not think she is capable of controlling herself and that she would be an easy make if given half the chance. This would be terrifying enough by itself, but when it is combined with the daughter's second realization, that she is beginning to experience powerful sexual feelings and would like to get involved, it is almost unbearable. She downgrades the fact that her sexual urges are normal and healthy.

Part of the child is deeply hurt by her parents' low estimation of her moral intent—she has done nothing. She is furious with the parents for their concern. The daughter may now become promiscuous to "show them." Or she may feel compelled to prove to Mother that she is virtuous. This often forces her into a relationship that leads to an early marriage. To be a married woman is to be a virtuous woman.

Let's look more closely at this marriage. What kind of a girl did the husband think he married? He chose a girl who probably presented herself as innocent, denied her sexual feelings, and tried to appear unsensuous. He was specifically drawn to the way she *appeared*. There has been a violation of the truth-in-packaging act here. The girl is not the shy, embarrassed girl she appears. She would like to be as sexually active as most people. Even though she marries a guy who is attracted to all the things Mother approved of, her true feelings have a way of expressing themselves. There's going to be trouble sooner or later when she is able to admit to her feelings and her husband doesn't know how to handle them.

If this marriage does deteriorate and if she wants to leave, the same old feelings of guilt that forced her to marry in the first place will return and in the same strength as before. Although she may have some good reasons to leave the marriage, she will feel guilty and unsure when these old feelings return.

As mentioned earlier, adolescents may choose careers wholly inappropriate to their needs. The child who follows a career in order to please a parent will feel constricted for being held back from what he wants. Not to please would be to risk being thought unworthy by the parents. A role that is forced upon a child causes him to feel angry and the anger makes him feel guilty. In order to feel less guilty, he works harder in his unpleasant role, but each attempt to change produces more guilt, causing the cycle to repeat. A person becomes trapped more in his anger and guilt than in his role.

Children from famous or very successful families often find themselves under pressure to uphold the family tradition. The fight here is more subtle. Rather than carrying the parents' hopes or becoming something merely to please, these children are measured by a standard of excellence that can be extremely frustrating. They are expected to succeed and to do well as a matter of course. Often, instead of praise, they hear a statement like, "Well, you had a smart mother and father," or "you *are* a Carlton." By going along with the family tradition they may grow to feel that little glory comes their way. This follows because they are often trying to fill the shoes of someone more talented.

Many of these people become highly respectable drudges. Few outsiders suspect that they are really unwilling workers who may hate what they do. Their pattern was set without their consent and they have little freedom to change. Superficially, they may be considered the freest people in society; in actuality, they are less free than most.

On the surface, their lives appear full, with their wide

variety of social activities, their wealth and their casualness toward success. We do not often appreciate how many of these traditions and social amenities are just part of a ritual. These rituals, like any that grow from a forced choice, were instituted to ward off feelings of anger and guilt over being trapped in a role.

Although there are social rules and limits, it is possible to act quite broadly within them, and certain kinds of behavior are accepted among the ranks of the prominent that would be regarded as decadent in the rest of society. Prominent people cling to their own rules and react to their breach with the same horror that the rest of us do to ours.

Although most of us are trapped to some extent, it is even more difficult to break out when one's way of life becomes ritualized, even if it is a broadly defined ritual dressed in luxury. People who travel in such a world, where everyone is monied or beautiful, spend much of their lives talking about the things other people do. They often do not *do* anything themselves. They may collect or sponsor people and their creations. To the extent that they ignore their own development, their lives are as meaningless and desperate as if they were trapped in a hated routine. They just do not have the excuse of not having enough money to postpone running away. They can afford to run away. They claim that they are free. They are not, really. They become trapped in keeping up appearances, and tradition, and they stay where they are. They, too, are afraid. They fear breaking with their rituals, their beautiful prison.

Other guilt-makers abound in our culture. While every family brings its own peculiar pressures to bear on its children, two common patterns developed in twentieth-century America that shook and shocked a large number of people.

The first evolved from the experience of immigrant parents in a new country and the other resulted from the hardship that parents lived through during the Great Depression. Each generated its own brand of guilt. Each forced the children to work in order to acquire things, but made them feel too guilty to enjoy what they had worked so hard to get.

We were all immigrants at one time in our family history. Many people today remember the relatives who immigrated and still can feel the tremors that this disruption had upon them. All people face a crisis when they immigrate. Because the new ways are strange, the immigrant misunderstands them and accepts and rejects them for superficial reasons. The ways of the old country are rigidly clung to out of fear. This failure to be flexible makes even fine old values appear ridiculous in the new setting. The first generation of children reject them as part of the rebellion of growing up. The immigrant often suffers a double loss. He feels disappointed at being excluded by the very society he hoped would save him and also by his children whom he loses to the new land and its customs.

The first generation children of immigrants often are even more at a loss. Even though the parents may feel rejected, they can remember a time when they were accepted. They have their memory of life in the old country to cling to. The backbreaking struggle to stay alive in this country is a reality for the immigrant, but it is part of his dream and he thinks about the old times for consolation. For the children it is different; there is suffering and exclusion without the memory of a better time. Instead, there are the tales of old men at the corner store who talk like your father and who also are made fun of like him. It is a hard beginning, and it is filled with a vague obligation to succeed by working, to set things straight, to prove that your father did not work for nothing.

The onrush from Eastern Europe is over but the effect of immigration is not. It is five-thirty in the afternoon and you have been standing in line since seven in the morning. A light snow is falling and there are halos around the lights on the pier. A heavy mist blurs the lights of New York across the harbor. You are Carlo DiFillipe and are five years old, tired and hungry, waiting to be let in. Finally, you and your family are herded to a gate and an immigration inspector scribbles something on your father's passport.

"How do you pronounce this name?" he asks. Your father doesn't answer. The inspector asks another man in uniform and writes down something on a piece of paper.

"Okay, Mr. Phillips," he says, patting your father on the back, "over there!"

Suddenly you are no longer the DiFillipe's but the Phillipses. Your father does not know what happened. Everything is so strange and fast. His friends tell him to keep the new name or else he will be sent back where he came from. None of them know any better than he, or even whom to ask.

After that your memories are of your father working hard at a laborer's job, coming home to collapse on the sofa, sometimes not being able to eat because of fatigue. He tells you that he made furniture in the old country, but you've never seen him work. You have to learn a new language and you become less like your father. There is little about him you want to be like. He kills himself with work. Bigots call names after him, and he doesn't know his way around as well as you do. Even some of his friends kid him about his name. It embarrasses you and makes you angry just to think about it. He seems so powerless here. It frightens you.

He tells you about the old ways, how it used to be. You're a wise guy, they say, just like your cousin Dominic whom you have never met. So you challenge your father and say, "If it was so great in the old country, what did you leave to come here for?" In those painful years it becomes clear to you that if you grow up to be like your parents, it is only going to make things hard for you.

You try to be accepted by the real Americans. It isn't easy for you, but it's easier than for your father. He couldn't speak the language. He was a foreigner. He was killing himself for you, so you could make it. That was the story you saw and heard. You had to work harder just to feel that you could look at yourself in the mirror at night without feeling ashamed. But no matter how hard you worked, you never felt good when your father came home and collapsed in the chair without supper. They had not only broken his back, they had taken all his hope.

You decided to make it, to go for broke. You fought to get a job, education, opportunity. Nothing came easy, but you were moving up. Maybe you learned a trade or started a small business. Soon you found yourself catching up, overcoming your handicaps. Soon the effort started to pay off. You became a *real* American yourself. You have the things you said you wanted: a home in "their" neighborhood, a membership in "their" country club. You played "their" sports and sported "their" taste in clothes, women, ethics and morality. You sent your kids to the best schools.

You tried to meet the best people, you tried to have the best of everything.

The shadows of the past were slow to fade, but if there was anyone in this world who could have done it, it was old Charlie Phillips. Tell the truth, Charlie: if that stupid immigration officer hadn't changed your name, you would have changed it yourself, right?

Now you are in your fifties, trying to keep your weight down by exercising regularly. Your wife is forty-eight, with the same sort of background as yourself. She won't be tied to the house like her poor mother. She's out a lot, a free woman, and you're proud of it. If only your mother could have had it so easy with all the time to do the things she wanted. All the time your wife has!

You are a happily married man. You stayed together through the rough times. Your wife was there when you needed her. Of course she has her problems. She can't keep a maid very long and gets moody, but all in all, there's nothing in your life that you feel can't be cured with a million dollars. Wouldn't that be nice?

You walk around your perfect Kentucky bluegrass lawn with its built-in sprinkler system and flagstone patio and wrought iron gazebo and think, "I really have made it. I have everything I ever wanted, everything my father never had. If only Pa could see this."

But it's just as well that the old man is gone. He would not be comfortable here. He would be afraid to touch anything, afraid he would break something. He might complain about the poor workmanship and just shrug. You'd get angry inside thinking "What does he know? Why can't he say something nice?" Even though you knew he would be proud of you, you would be able to detect a note of criticism. He worked all his life and had nothing, and you have everything. How you pity the poor bastard! How your wife pities her poor mother and dreads looking old, fat and beaten like her. It's tough to think about. What's more, you find it a little difficult relaxing here yourself, thinking you should be doing something else. You find it difficult relaxing anywhere. You must work, acquire, be like "them."

Your father was a stranger in a strange land. He did not know its customs, its language or its ways, but he knew where he came from, and he was not unknown to himself. He was torn from the land he knew and thrown into a new world. But what he was taken from could not be taken from him. He had memories of a childhood, of a manhood in another land where he was accepted for what he was because everyone was like him.

He knew instinctively that he was as good as the next man, because he was as good as the people he came from. He was perhaps bolder than his friends, willing to risk immigrating, leaving his country for your future. Yet by leaving his native soil, he robbed you of a national identity to share in common with him, a sense of belonging to the same thing.

In order to fit in, you had to reject many of the things that set him apart in this new land, often the very things that gave him his sense of strength, his sense of identity, and allowed him to survive. He was not just a beaten man collapsing after work each day. That was the way you saw him. He was a man with a past, a man with a perspective you would never know, a man who could fit the present into its appropriate place.

You are the real foreigner. You have become a stranger

to yourself in a land you know all too well. Your past was forged out of the pressing crowds at the subway station at five-thirty, of the bloody noses you got on the way home from school for being different. You accepted the things you thought you needed to get ahead here. You aspired to values sometimes just because they were the opposite of the values that caused your family to be rejected—not because they were good. You became the best that you could put together from your fragmented encounter with a society that frightened you and threatened to reject you unless you became one of "them."

Your memories are the memories of making it. The values are of being successful. The identity is in how well you have done and what you are. That's not bad, is it? Is it? Look at you. You have become trapped in a world you still don't fully understand. You have no choice but to struggle to get more. The identity you have chosen is the identity of acquiring what your father never had. Your father never had anything, you feel. So, you are doomed to chase after everything in the world even if you never find your own self.

Your wife struggles to be different from her mother, to see that her children do not slip and to expose some clue to that unhappy past. If you were somehow forced to leave this country and immigrate to another land, where could you go? You would be a stranger in any land, even in your father's old village. You would have to bring your collection of "things" with you because in some way "things" become your only identity. They won't fit on the ship. You would be lost without them. Your children have rejected your materialistic identity and are out looking for a new one, one much like your father's, the one you rejected before. What *are* the values you live by? Why won't your kids accept them?

Millions of Americans are trapped in this maze of self-defeating acquisition. They feel pressured to move out to the suburbs, to erect their own little fortresses against the world, filled with treasures to console them. When they do relax for a moment, the image of that poor old man barely getting to the top of the stairs, collapsing in the chair, comes across their dozing eyes. Or they see their struggling mother, the baby machine, the cook, the pessimistic endurer waiting for things to get better, which they never did in time for her to enjoy. They may feel better that they have escaped, but still feel under pressure, and, yes, guilty for having survived.

Beyond the pressure to be part of the system that rejected your parents and to acquire material things is the need to justify a father's years of hard work outside a system that would not let him in. So you work as hard as possible. Failure to work, failing to fulfill the role for which the immigrant parents toiled is to make their struggle appear in vain. Work redeems your parents' memory. So, you feel guilty when you're not working. Guilty enjoying the things they never had.

Women feel they must live a life where they are pampered and taken care of, even when they would rather be doing something interesting. Life is lived as a memorial to the good works of the parents, commemorating their self-sacrifice. To give up the effort, to abandon the system is almost a sacrilege, a dishonor, debasing of their memory. It's a disgrace to fail.

The children of immigrants are not free. Before they can break away from their constant work they must understand that *it was not their fathers who were most deprived but themselves.* If, after a few years here, father and son immigrated again, the son would find himself the worse off. The father would still have a sense of who he was and the ability to enjoy himself, to savor the good times in life without guilt. The children of immigrants took the acquisition of material things as their identity. They could not accept what their fathers had to offer. In time, as their fortune grew, they were able to convince themselves that it was their father who lacked things. They direct their energy to having more than he did. Their identity is that of someone who must work to death. It is this image that always comes back to haunt them. It is this image that keeps them in the rat race, because to stop is to have no identity at all.

If the immigrant and his children seem depressing, the source of guilt that they generate as parents is at least clear. Families who were exposed to the Great Depression were subject to influences just as painful but less obvious.

The depression is hard to imagine for those who did not live through it. Psychologically, it cut a wide and relentless swath through the self-confidence of an entire world, leaving a heritage of pessimism and doubt. Worst of all, it created the belief that nothing good was ever permanent, and sometime, when least expected, fate would take away everything one had worked for and come to depend on. A major depression, like an earthquake, is indiscriminate. The economic earthquake of the thirties wiped out people regardless of race, religion, or any of the other categories that people seem to fall into when other people need someone to hate. Everyone was hurt. Nothing anyone did, no group that one belonged to, no amount of fortune was insulation enough. Many of the traditional beliefs that people had about safeguarding the future were undermined. There was little that people could any longer believe in, not as an absolute. Nothing, it seemed, could save someone when there was a depression. People with extensive educations were reduced to cleaning streets if they were lucky. Businessmen sold apples. Nothing made sense any more.

The people raising families at this time suffered the worst. Bare survival was the issue that occupied all their thoughts. Get a job, any job, keep it and save. The children had to have a chance. Something happened to these people, something never to be erased from their minds. In later years they would tell anyone who would listen, even in the midst of some great success, that one should not be too sure about anything, that the time for enjoying things is still not yet.

Today, sitting at a full table, they remember the hungry years and take pride in enjoying hard crusts of bread or saving things they might be able to use some day. The depression seems to be with them all the time. It never loses its grip.

"You don't know what it was like," they tell their children.

They tell them that, and they are wrong. They tell them that if they had known then what they know now, things would have been very different. They would have been able to take chances, make changes in their lives and survive the depression without festering memories. But, in truth, they knew *everything* then that they know now except for one thing. They did not know the way things would eventually turn out. What stops us also stopped them: our fear of the future, our doubts about ourselves.

Today's children may not remember any of the events or the struggle firsthand, but they know how it feels because they have been taught to feel it and to live it as if it were part of their own life. It has become part of the children's lives because it has never been far from their parents'.

Growing up in an atmosphere of futility and pessimism generates fear at any prospect of change because all change is expected to be for the worse until proven otherwise. To leave a job, a stable home, any known thing, no matter how irritating, how ingratiating or demanding it might be, for something unknown, is viewed with near panic—even if it seems better. To risk change is to tempt fate. Parents warn their children to take it easy, to be careful, to make sure they know what they're doing, not to rush into anything. These parents lived life as a series of potential horrors and were so thankful when some fear did not materialize that they forgot completely that fear had paralyzed them so they could not move ahead.

Not moving backward felt like moving ahead. And if you knew all they knew, you wouldn't smile.

For some historians the depression ended sometime in the thirties, but for these people it never ended. They carried around with them the glowering pessimism that had broken them. They kept it as a house pet, to watch after the children, especially when shopping.

The depression gave new meanings to words like "should" and "ought to" and "must." A sense of duty and obligation, a sense of work before pleasure, was woven through every sensible garment manufactured and purchased during these years. The practical aspect of life was the only one worth discussing. Some people did indulge themselves, but they were considered foolish, silly, or irresponsible. They would pay the price some day, just wait! Children were told to fear giving in to feelings, to work hard and put something away. Only after a while it became clear that there would never, ever, really be enough saved away. There would never be enough to take it easy and enjoy life. Enjoy life? Children were told you can only enjoy life when you are sure that you are secure from the depression returning, and no one was saved in the last one. Somewhere there was an evil eye, a curse, a hex, something without a name waiting to take away your worldly possessions.

The lesson that people who survived the depression taught their children was that you could never be sure about your happiness. Indeed, as they saw things, they were right, but did not know why. They saw happiness as material security, not as self-fulfillment. Material security, the goal of the new immigrant, very often the one most hurt in the depression, was the only thing they knew. If they lost this, they felt they lost everything. Because of their emphasis on work and achievement, their children were led into practical careers, jobs, security. They were led away from discovering themselves. And the irony of it all is that the goals they were led away from, their talents, their hobbies, were the only goals that another depression could not take away from them! The careers they struggled to achieve were just as vulnerable to another depression as their parents were.

The child born since the atomic bomb was born with the fear of losing his life and so, believing his death is imminent, he plans to live. The child born and brought up during the depression was brought up with the fear that some unknown force was going to reduce him to poverty, and so he lives to work. Poverty is a more powerful fear for these people than death, because death to them is something remote while the monster that killed their parents' spirit now sleeps under *their* kitchen table threatening *them*.

These people are all but bound to feel guilty when they do something for pleasure because their self-denial, their gloom and perpetual timidity have made all things seem futile. They looked at pleasure the way they were forced to look at so many things: something nice, but they could learn to do without it. The object of parental training in the depression was to teach good manners, efficient toilet habits and to learn to do without almost anything.

Where in the sea of your parents' friends are the people who splurged, who spent money on themselves? Do you remember anyone with a red convertible in the thirties, a swashbuckling ladies man, or someone who had a sailboat? You may remember one or two, but if you remember many people, your family was very unusual. Whom did *you* have to show you how to enjoy yourself? Your parents had forgotten how to play. One had fun on special days. Every purchase had to have a reason, a good sensible reason. It was rare for them to buy something for themselves. The way things were would just not permit it—anyway they got along without it before.

No other generation of Americans received such a mixed bag of gifts from their parents as those who were born between 1920 and 1940. Part of the inheritance was the drive and industry to work, to pull out of the black pit. This was coupled with a disarming pessimism that revealed itself at the most embarrassing and destructive times. Fear over taking a chance or making a change was ever to plague them. Work, work, work was the cry that they heard from the monster under the kitchen table, sometimes even waking them up from sleep at night. Finally some part of them accepted the idea that work was good in and of itself. This obsession for work without considering what work meant besides being employed, produced a strange and self-defeating result. You had to have a job, any job!

The harder some people worked, the less they got out of it. They produced less and were decidedly less creative. The more they advanced in a particular job, the less they seemed to accomplish. It was not merely a matter of them growing less able to handle the work as they moved up the ladder. They were removed from what they really enjoyed, from the things they were most suited for. They were not able to tap their best resources and talents. The goal had become to work and to advance, even if their interests and needs were not met.

In the cycle of acquiring and achieving that characterizes people trapped in this struggle, a point is often reached where a person can feel comfortable doing what he is doing. He can handle his work and even enjoy it. More than that— he may be doing something he finds fulfilling. Too often people move past this point, thinking that they will be happier somewhere else. As a result, people only find more stress, more work unsuited to their personality and abilities. They long for the time before when they felt in charge of themselves.

It's not belaboring the obvious to say that it's as important to know when you are happy as when you are not. You may want to go back to that happier situation someday.

Much of the pressure to achieve is generated by the American culture. It is a common observation of Americans who travel abroad for the first time to notice how much more content some Europeans are with simple occupations. Waiters seem pleased to be waiting on them in Paris, barbers seem to take pride in their work in Rome, bellboys in London have been pleased to be at their job for years and do not have plans to go to night school to become a hotel manager. We seem to have lost much of our ability to accept ourselves in America. The pressure to be better, to be smarter, to be richer is so great that few of us have ever taken the time just to be good at something we enjoy and to enjoy something just because we are good at it.

We drive into a service station to have a repair made and find that the man at the pump doesn't understand what we're talking about because he only quit his job at the supermarket last week. The "mechanic" is just working part-time and will have a look at it. The owner of the station, one of a chain, says "No"; another place will have to take care of it because his chain doesn't make any money on that sort of repair. Anyway, the owner doesn't know anything about fixing cars. He's a businessman. What's wrong with being a good mechanic and liking it? What happened to all those guys I used to know in high school who used to love to tear cars apart and build them again? Did they have to go into engineering? And if they did, how many of them are hating all that paperwork?

There is a belief in our culture that every intelligent person should have an academic education and an intellectual career. Yet many brilliant discoveries have been made by people who have taken time off and returned to an easier, simpler life. We're hung up not only by the depression but also by another bit of history: America was made up of people who were discontent with what they had. Both wanted more!

An entire generation of Americans between forty and sixty finds it difficult to relax and enjoy themselves. They have all the trappings of success, the homes, the clubs, the appearances, but they are caught on a treadmill and stop on the golf course trying to remember what they're "supposed" to be doing instead. They live their way of life not so much because they want to, but because it is a way of paying back the parents for their struggle and self-denial. The hard work of the children of the depression has produced the greatness that we call America.

Perhaps no group of people feel so advantaged and so triumphant in their material accomplishments as these people do. Yet there is a tentative quality to their victory, a postponement of pleasure and, most of all, a dread of anything that suggests change.

How do you explain to a father who suffered through the depression so you could go to school and become a lawyer that the idea really wasn't yours, that you want to quit and train horses? He will recoil at the idea and recite a list of the possible things that will go wrong. He will tell you to make sure you have all the "basics" in life before you make a choice. The basics include almost everything except things that you do because you like to do them. Pleasure is not a basic in life—so you were told and you believed it.

This perverted philosophy of life has drained the energy

and life out of millions of people who sit among collections of material things that they supposedly wanted more than anything else in the world at the time. That's why they worked so hard for them and denied themselves. If those things are so important to them, why aren't they really happy? Why, when they see a hippie walking barefoot in the park, do they get angry about the way kids are today and then become so upset with themselves that they can't take off their own shoes and play in the fountain? In spite of all they have, they feel trapped.

The philosophy of overwork has systematically robbed us of our youth—not the years, but our belief that it is possible at any time to do anything we really want to do. There is nothing you can't have if you are willing to work at it, we were told; except maybe peace of mind in finding ourselves. As soon as we believe that there is no other road open except the one we are on, we begin to slow down. Why? Because on that road there is only one end: the funeral service. Because we fear that end, we feel hopeless, produce less, enjoy fewer things in the world and whimper off to our deaths.

You do not have to do it. I mean it. You do not have to sit reading this book and say, "But I can't change." The fact is you can. You can really do something. There is time left if you begin now. There is time left to find something.

You are going to have to cope with one more kind of guilt before you make a change, and that is the guilt that comes from hurting other people. People *will* be hurt if you change. From what I mentioned earlier it follows that for some people your break will be seen as a sign of your foolishness, or of your letting them down, or of your showing your selfishness. For others it will bring up their fear of being outgrown, of losing your contribution to their lives or the fear of having to face up to similar feelings in themselves. But that is not the result of your action. It is the result of their own fears. Why not let that be their problem? You have enough problems of your own. You don't need to go on feeling the guilt that someone else has left to you. It's time to get rid of that household pet under the kitchen table.

Really, why should you feel guilty about doing what you want? You aren't about to hurt anyone intentionally! You are responsible. You've got years of selfless service to prove that. How long do you have to serve before your sentence is complete? Where is it decreed that you must spend the rest of your life doing what you are doing, being what you are, if you don't want to? Maybe what you're doing is all wrong. Maybe it's really someone else's needs you're fulfilling. How much do you want? If you can't be happy with the material things you have now, you probably can't be happy with anything. Maybe it's time you did stop running after all and stopped feeling guilty about it. There is a way to be happy, but it seems you can't get there the way you're going.

The way to overcome the guilts that are tied to the past begins with understanding them and where they came from. It is not enough to recognize the sources of guilt in your life but it is also important to see how guilt affects what you do. This takes time and effort but is well worth it. The next time you want to do something and find yourself putting it off because you don't feel right about it, stop what you are doing and think about it.

Where did the veto come from? Whose voice was it? Do you have to listen to it?

The inhibition of enjoyment has been so common in many people's lives that they do not even notice when it happens.

No, it's not at all hopeless. What is hopeless is to expect that change will be painless and that there will not be discouragements along the way. I think change can be a great deal easier if you are aware of the kinds of problems that exist before you try. This is not meant to discourage you from trying, but only to make the chances of success much greater when you do. If you become aware of the problems you'll face, including the feelings of guilt that have held you back, you'll be able to find a way through them. Be patient and have courage. It all takes a little time. And there is quite a bit more you still need to find out.

8

WHAT'S WORSE: FAILURE OR SUCCESS?

Many of the obstacles that keep people from doing what they really want, or force them to do things they really dislike, are, as I have shown, invented by the people themselves. That is precisely what makes them difficult to remove. It is much easier to recognize someone else's attempt to thwart you and to struggle against it; but when you yourself are the stumbling block, it is much more difficult, even if the obstacle is no more formidable.

Some obstacles are not self-made, such as physical handicaps. I am more concerned with how people use obstacles as excuses than the obstacles themselves. Even with severe handicaps, some people manage to do quite well. Others with very small problems use their difficulties as their excuse for failing. This is not to say that small barriers are not real or that they do not affect us. But if we want to, we find that somehow we can get around them even if we cannot always get over them.

You may not be able to find what you want where you are now. Many of us are like the fool looking for a lost coin under a street lamp many feet away from where it dropped; he is looking there because the light is better. We have to look where the things we want can be found. Not looking in the right place is the first obstacle.

Behind this self-defeating behavior—placing imaginary barriers in the way, wearing blinders and the rest—is usually an attempt to avoid self-confrontation. And when people are afraid to see themselves they're likely to work toward the wrong goal. An unsatisfying success in a field that means little to a person may be a way to avoid risk or possible failure in another field that would mean a great deal.

Lowell is a thirty-eight-year-old lawyer with the best education and training who comes from a prominent attorney's family. There was much conflict at home when he was growing up; he and his father never got along well. His self-made father was such a strong personality that Lowell could never deal with him; he always felt beaten and vanquished. He gave up his wish to study classics, entered and excelled in law school, clerked for a Supreme Court Justice and joined a prestigious law firm that Lowell's father regarded as snobbish. He married a girl from the same social circle as his senior partners. He struggled to get out of his father's social world, a world that he came to regard as confining and stifling, but tried to make a success at the same career.

In a few years Lowell became respected in the law firm for his dogged thoroughness and his ability to dig out the facts of a case and put them in order. He could be absolutely fearsome in his deployment of legal weaponry and facts. When he prepared a case for one of the senior partners, he was a formidable weapon and a treacherous adversary to face in court.

His declarations to the contrary notwithstanding, Lowell did not seem to feel at ease in his job. He complained of severe stomach upsets much of the time. He was worst on days before he was to go into court. He would sleep poorly and perspire so profusely at these times that the sheets had to be changed in the middle of the night. He would begin the day by trying to retch. He found it impossible to get any food down and vomited several times during the day.

During court sessions he was alert to the point of exhaustion. He took extensive notes and cross-checked them against pages of outlines and citations that drove his secretaries crazy. He had his finger on every point of law and rarely was overruled when he cited a precedent. When he *was* overruled and one of his questions ordered struck, he became anxious and furious and almost immediately nauseated.

In spite of his dramatic and comprehensive use of all his legal skills, Lowell was so uncomfortable taking on cases entirely by himself that he usually refused them. He could follow assignments perfectly and prepared the material so well that all a senior partner needed to do at the trial was to follow Lowell's typewritten plan. It was usually flawless. Yet as his responsibilities grew and he was given more to do on his own, he became increasingly restless and unsure of himself. His best work was still done when he was working for one of the senior partners and had to report to someone. The less intelligent, the less skillful the senior partner, the better was Lowell's performance. He would fight with the partners, challenge them even on minor points and then do brilliant research to prove himself right. Everything that Lowell did looked like an attempt to make a fool out of the senior partner in the name of thoroughness.

Lowell became a valuable and powerful member of the law firm. He intimidated many of the partners, but they found his work indispensable. Understandably, they were at first unwilling to make him a full partner and held him at bay for some time. The resulting frustration only increased Lowell's energies and his work became even more brilliant if excruciatingly painful for the partners to tolerate. He had his hand on every reachable detail. He was, to his mind, the only competent one in the firm. It was often necessary to hold him back to contain his zeal. He made the others feel inept.

Lowell was finally made a partner and given his own area of responsibility. The partners felt that if he was trying so hard for others, he would work harder with no restraints and would be less of a nuisance. Immediately after becoming a partner a very strange thing happened. Lowell's performance began to sag miserably. He was no longer able to develop extensive and thorough trial plans, and he found the prospect of going into court paralyzing. When previously he fought like a tiger to overcome the partners who did the trial work, he now felt weak. He found he could not do the job himself and could not face the judge at all. He watched helplessly as his output declined, and resigned his partnership within the first year to take a position as a junior with a bigger law firm.

Lowell was trapped by his own inability to deal with his feelings, especially his lingering anger at his father and people who, like father, wielded authority. He saw the senior partners as safe targets for his anger which he could disguise as hard work. Since the partners symbolized his own father, he never felt comfortable getting angry at them directly; instead, he got to them with his self-torturing thoroughness, i.e. by being too perfect a "son." The possibility of getting out of control caused him unbearable anxiety which manifested itself in sleeplessness and stomach complaints. Lowell was always on the verge of letting his anger break through, and this kept him in a state of panic.

All he could count on to keep him in check was the senior partners acting to subdue him. Although he was not aware of this, he certainly depended on it. Much of his life was an attempt to prove to his father that he was worthwhile and to conceal his anger at his father for thinking him worthless. There was little room for anything else.

Real success in life was not possible for Lowell because he was always trying to prove his worth. If he did succeed in reaching the top and held a position where he alone was responsible for himself, he would panic, fearful that he would lose control of his anger. Rather than be a free agent, rather than be the boss, he was forced to function at a much lower level than his ability permitted.

In spite of his excellent work, he would always be dependent upon another, older man to keep him in control. He could not be creative on his own or even be forceful. Everything he did had to be directed toward a substitute for his father. His energies were so drained by maintaining the old unsettled conflicts that there was little strength left over to reach the goal he wanted. Moreover, to reach that goal—being a classics professor—he would first have had to become less dynamic, less materialistic, less a man of the world; that is: less of what his father was. This change would have been a terrible threat to him because he would have had to appear like all the things his father accused him of being—weak, passive, lacking drive.

Lowell could never be the successful lawyer his father was. Any success that Lowell would find would ultimately depend on values that his father demeaned. Lowell will *never* be completely acceptable in his father's eyes *and this is his father's problem*. To know this, causes great pain. But unless these false goals are given up, there is no hope for real achievement on Lowell's terms.

A long string of accomplishments is not always success.

Other people shun success for other reasons. Many who feel trapped in an unsatisfying situation stay there because it offers them a haven of sorts. Like Lowell, some prefer to remain unexposed and hide behind the skirts of someone else's authority. While they do not like to be told what to do, they like it even less to be held accountable. They fear making mistakes if they were on their own.

One powerful reason why people do not succeed is that they are afraid of failing. Everybody knows that success requires effort. And yet, everyone also knows people who try hard, do succeed and are nevertheless miserable. How is that explained?

People who do succeed and still are miserable—like Lowell until he demoted himself—have just not succeeded at the right task. Lowell will probably push himself to the same point in the new law firm, but until he seeks what he originally wished for himself, the life of a classics professor, he will not be able to find a rewarding success.

People like Lowell find it easier to succeed at a goal that does not represent what they want in life, because it is more painful to fail at what is really important to them. Lowell would dread doing badly in classics. Some failures in the law would upset him, but he would find them tolerable.

Often people who appear to be crucially involved and to have much at stake are only committing part of themselves to the effort—the part about which they feel least vulnerable. Their success sometimes is made possible because they feel free to take chances and believe that they have little to lose. Success is usually more difficult for people who are not doing what they want.

It is not uncommon to hear students at exam time saying, "I only got a B, but I didn't study. If I'd studied, I would have gotten an A." This deceptive logic is protection against failure. Although it is more obvious, it is really no different from the sour grapes we use to maintain self-esteem when we don't succeed.

Too many people are unwilling to commit themselves to fulfilling their dreams because failure would mean the loss of all their hopes. Countless secret composers, artists, dancers, decorators, dressmakers, writers, innkeepers, farmers, travelers, students, waste their lives doing something they hate but that provides a safe haven for them, for even if they fail, it really doesn't matter to their innermost selves.

Others are aware of a hidden wish or talent and *do* try to fulfill it but do not try very hard. Since their effort is halfhearted, they do not often succeed. They use the same excuse as the student who "could have gotten an A" if he'd bothered to study; they say they didn't really try because they didn't have the time or the circumstances weren't right. Actually, they failed because they were afraid of failing, not because they didn't have the time or right conditions. After that experience they are less willing to try.

They fear getting hurt again. Their dreams go underground.

Self-development does take time, but anybody who cuts out busy-work will find many hours in the week to accomplish much. But you must be willing to try. Many great writers took menial, untaxing jobs while they worked hard and long at their own creative projects at night and during lunch hours. Others who have taken unpleasant jobs because of the promise of money find they need to reward themselves with extra relaxation: coffee breaks, long lunches, or several drinks when they get home. The work gets stretched out. The unpleasantness of the job makes it necessary to lose time unwinding. This in turn makes it more difficult to find the time to develop other talents.

The energy left over from obligations is often insufficient to propel us to try to discover our talents or to succeed even when we sometimes do try. And if we are disappointed in our performance, we begin to doubt whether we are any good at all. Any motivation that might have existed is now diminished and future efforts are discouraged.

That failure can result from such unfavorable circumstances as insufficient time, low levels of available energy, and underdeveloped talents and skills is to be expected. At the beginning of any undertaking, even with favorable conditions on one's side, including youth and pre-occupying zeal, the possibility of failure is a constant companion. It is only later, when the struggle has been under way for some time and the rough spots smoothed by experience and effort, that success becomes more frequent. Even then temporary failures are common, but the memory of previous successes and the self-confidence built over years of winning out over adverse results gives one the strength to try again.

We really cannot judge ourselves when we begin something new, because we probably don't understand enough about the venture. We can decide, however, what we liked doing if we did try. That alone is good reason to continue in the beginning. When we like what we do, the work becomes easier. We look forward to it, make time available for it. When we find a cause we can learn to love, we get an unexpected dividend. We learn to love ourselves more. Developing any ability requires a full emotional commitment even if you can only work at it part-time. A few hours a week can be enough to find yourself if you do not waste them.

Becoming committed to the task of self-development and self-discovery also requires looking at yourself in a new way. A housewife, for example, must stop seeing herself as everyone's personal maid and resenting the fact. She must take herself seriously as, for example, an interior decorator or at least as a student in interior decorating, and begin. She must see her present situation as it really is. It may be a way of keeping peace, a way of making ends meet, or like Lowell, a way of solving some old conflict by acting it out in the present day situation. You must begin to think of yourself as becoming the person you want to be.

Failing too soon is simply another way of avoiding this self-confrontation. The change from failure to success is a matter of attitude and commitment. Once the present circumstances are recognized as temporary substitutes or as elaborate obstacles or just safe, they become expendable. The school teacher who is bored with the same routine every day must gather her courage and perhaps join the Peace Corps to feel that her contribution is important again. A bank teller must take some risk and give up his financial security (and some of his self-hatred for staying at a job he dislikes so much) to accept the insecurities and freedoms of being a fishing guide, if that's what he really wants. As one's abilities in one's special area are given the time, effort and the full impact of one's emotional investment, they grow. Once a person says, "This is who I really am, what I am all about, what I was really meant to do," it is easier to decide how to spend one's time. It feels natural; it feels right. If you are patient, you will begin to make gains, and you will start to break away from the old routine.

This marks the beginning of the big breakthrough for you. Once you make a commitment and begin to follow it through, the entire world will change for you. And you will be able to see that for years you tried to find satisfaction at something that wasn't really you. The harder you worked, the less you liked it. It is as if you had been trying to put a square peg into a round hole—by pushing harder. You couldn't have been as blind as all that, could you?

Look how much more pleasurable it is when you do something that fits you. You work much more rapidly and perform better. You are able to concentrate because what you are working on is a part of you. We are all egocentric, every last one of us, and rather than fight this fact we should utilize it. It's easier to work at something because it is important to you than because you are going to be judged. When you play a role, you are measured by how well you comply to someone else's standards. When you do something on your own, you care only how much you fulfill your own expectations.

When you work at something you like, you do put in less effort and get out more reward. This may sound impossible and go against everything you have been taught (or society reinforces), but I assure you it is true. If you become involved in your own special world you will probably spend more time there because you enjoy it. Even though you may work more intensively, you do not work harder. You do less that is irrelevant. You don't spend your time trying to whittle the edges off the square pegs so that they fit into those blasted round holes. You fit naturally into what you are doing; what you are doing is you.

No one would try to teach a duck to catch mice or a cat how to swim. Unless you own a traveling side show and want to display these animals as freaks, it just isn't worth the effort. How many of us, if we really looked at where our natural abilities lie and compared them to what we are doing in life, would be better off than some soaking wet cat receiving some catnip and a pat on the head from his master for a short swim across a tank? It's a horrible way for a cat to spend its life. Are any of us better off when we do things we hate only for the reward at the end? That's a pretty horrible way for any human to spend his life.

Another consequence of becoming committed is that one's problems in general also seem less forbidding. When people are unhappy playing a role, they look for relief elsewhere in their lives. If a role is unrewarding, then a hobby or a sport may be forced to take on the burden of providing the completeness that life lacks. People who are unhappy in their role contaminate everything they touch with this feeling. As their displeasure grows, their need for success in the hobby or sport increases. Other people begin to take on added importance. Spouses and friends are called upon increasingly to bolster their spirits. As the importance of their role decreases, so does the enjoyment of life in general. Eventually, their hobbies, sports and the responses of friends help very little. People become hurt and angry at their failures in other undertakings that were substitutes for fulfilling themselves.

When a commitment to a goal is finally made, and effort is expended to achieve something meaningful, the pressure is taken off everyone. People can play golf for fun again. Spouses can be themselves again. There is no great need for them to be super-humans who make their spouse feel worthwhile. Feeling worthwhile is your own job.

When a commitment is made, there is more energy available to enjoy other people, to listen and to hear and understand more of the world. The world becomes more pertinent because events are related to something you are doing, something you see as worthwhile and constructive. You see a new order of importance around you. You have more patience and feel more secure about yourself. It is something that has to be experienced in order to be believed. In discovering yourself, you discover a new world.

Some people—like lawyer Lowell—have little control over their feelings. They may change jobs and life styles but often the same patterns begin to reappear in the new role they choose. Their goal is not to attain something real but something privately symbolic. Like Lowell, they seek to prove something, not please themselves. When they do succeed, they often find they are still miserable. They do not do things for their own sake—only for what they symbolize.

There is another side to doing what one really wants. If you do become involved in something you really like, something very close to you and to what you really stand for, you are exposed to being hurt. You are vulnerable.

If, after putting off a career in singing, a housewife begins lessons again only to find she is not as good as she thought she was, she is in for a very severe disappointment. In addition to being told by her husband that she burned dinner, she will be told by her voice coach that the shrill quality in her upper register ruins her performance. Her voice is a part of her. It is her spirit, her life, her investment. She is being attacked. The injury is deep and painful. Steps must be taken to deal with this. She must do vocal exercises to improve. If they fail, she must favor her voice by singing only what she does best. The hurt, more real than anything anyone ever said about her tuna fish casserole, gnaws at her. It is at this vulnerable point that people begin to make strides and begin to show true growth. It is also at this time when people decide to quit and return to something safer.

When you make a commitment, stay with it. You will find that you are not as good as you hoped you were, but not as bad as you feared.

Once people do become involved, to begin to find themselves, some rather surprising changes occur. People come to be regarded differently. Old prejudices change because they have often grown out of self-discontent. Some of the old fears about the effects that a change would bring prove meaningless. It no longer seems necessary to give up everything in order to be what one secretly wanted. In fact, the fear that one would have to give up so much now appears like a flimsy excuse for not putting oneself on the line in the first place.

It was a way of making the odds look too long. It was a way to rationalize staying where you were.

Now it probably doesn't seem vital any more to make drastic changes in everything. Is a move to a distant country really crucial to the total plan? It may not be necessary to call a lawyer and arrange for a divorce. The severe consequences that the children would supposedly suffer by your change do not seem to materialize. They are actually happier because you are happier. The fears that the world would fall apart if you changed were nothing more than your excuse to keep yourself in your place, to allow you to feel justified in not taking a risk.

In the end, the risk does not seem so great. So many of your fears were not justified. They were fears that came from inside you and then projected onto the world. Your thoughts that certain people would hold you back from finding yourself may have been thoughts with which you held yourself back. Once you are committed, others need no longer be regarded as obstacles to your success. Now they may even be able to offer you something to help you on your way.

While it is true that the person who has made a commitment and a change can fail in his new effort, it is also true that he is now in more command and can take action to remedy things if and when they go wrong. When he does succeed, it is his own special triumph. Sometimes it is necessary to discover ourselves before we are able to see the rest of the world undistorted.

Success and perception of the world depend upon success and perception within ourselves. The first step on the journey to personal freedom is always a journey within ourselves.

9

LEAVING
THE DIRTY WORK
TO SOMEONE ELSE

How do people make the decisions that affect the rest of their lives?

Because it is so serious, so important and concerns so many people, one would expect people to give the decision a great deal of thought, to examine every side of the question—especially the things they stand to gain, the things they are afraid to lose—and then to devise some careful plan that would allow them to make the change as easily as possible with the best chances for success.

That is what one would logically expect, but that is not what happens. Man is not a logical animal. He is paradoxical, impulsive, outrageously self-punitive and self-defeating. He acts on incomplete evidence to fulfill fantasies he does not really understand. However, his disorganization and confusion in examining all of the possibilities are only minor faults compared to the indirect route he frequently takes toward his first break from his accustomed life style.

What force allows him to change his life? Does it come

from quiet reflection, from pondering the issues? No! Man is an oblique animal, frequently unable to act directly on his own internal feelings. He is accustomed to using the external world as his excuse for not doing what he wanted. It is only in keeping with this habit that when he finally makes his decision, he often does so as the result of an external event, even fate. Sometimes the external event that allows him to decide is within his control. Even if he reacts to other people, he has often made them do his dirty work. Leaving the dirty work to others is usually a rotten thing to do.

Marriage partners commonly do many things to force each other to leave—maneuvers that are not recognized for what they are.

Although gaining weight and losing one's physical attractiveness may have other meanings, it is often a passive-hostile act directed against the spouse. The fat partner, getting fatter, may say things like, "I'm afraid I'm going to lose you," which is often the unspoken wish. The other partner tries to be reassuring, but eventually gets pushed into looking elsewhere for consolation. In the process he may become the active disrupter of the marriage and feel guilty and miserable about it. He eventually consoles himself by lying that he had no other choice. The fat partner can claim she couldn't help it. Yes, the role of the fat unattractive spouse is usually played by women. When it is played by men, it is less frequently the reason for change because the woman is less likely to take action against this sort of husband.

Becoming a drunkard or compulsive gambler is another way of passively inciting the partner to action. Again, like all passive roles, it produces large amounts of anger and again the familiar call is heard, "But I can't help it."

Becoming ineffective on the job and then getting fired is still another way of calling external forces into play. Incompetence at work is not a specific symptom of a particular kind of problem; it is a general way that people use to back out of a situation.

All these destructive activities have one thing in common. All are ways of saying, "I am angry with you." They are a perverted way of saying "I am angry" because somehow the angry person is unable to express anger without first putting himself in a position where he already appears to be punished, i.e., fired, obese, depressed, ulcer-ridden or alcoholic. How could anyone possibly get angry at someone who has brought so much misery upon his own head? The answer: it is very easy to get angry at someone who brings misery upon himself. We do it all the time. It does make us feel very frustrated and even guilty.

People who punish themselves are enormously angry in the first place or else they wouldn't be punishing themselves. Knowing that, one needs to figure out who they are angry at. If you are married to such a person, the chances are that he is also angry at you. If he is not angry at you but at what you have come to represent (symbolically) in your marriage, then, to some extent, he is really angry at someone in his past and is taking it out on you. If that is the case, then (and to the same extent) you are not completely real to him. You are an image derived from his past. Your needs are going to be fulfilled only by chance in such a relationship, not by the other person's direct intent. How could you get what you want if the other person really doesn't see you as you? The chances are that in some way you are doing the same sort of thing to him.

For example, a husband who came from a home with a cruel and vindictive mother finds fault with his wife in public. Years ago, he found it difficult to be angry at his mother because it made him feel so guilty and because mother was so punitive. Now he uses his wife as a safe target for his anger. His criticisms (although always founded in fact) are never important enough for his wife to make a fuss about. It is the day after day, week after week, onslaught of his complaints that finally begins to take their toll on her. When she eventually blows up at him, he feels that he is right, that she is entirely wrong and over-reacting. He feels justified in getting angry at her. She puts up with all this because she herself had difficulties when she was a child, but with her father. He was strict and controlling and made her account for everything she did. She expressed her anger at her father by becoming wild and delinquent, but it made her feel so uncomfortable about herself that she sought out the same sort of person to punish her. The husband married someone to be his whipping boy. The wife married someone to whip her. People like this usually back into decisions.

The great American pastime of throwing oneself into one's work is another way of forcing a marriage to the brink. Except here the super-worker is able to say, "I am doing it all for you and the kids." We have seen how people work to punish themselves, but some people overwork to stay away from the family. If you love your family so much but are knocking yourself out so you never get a chance to see them, maybe you should change your job instead of making your family feel guilty. Anyway, everyone knows you're not doing it for them. You're doing it for you. Just so we all understand each other.

Another way of using external events to make your decision is to get other people to do your dirty work. This tactic has special appeal because it does not require much self-appraisal and gets other people to play the role of the heavy. Failing in life and getting your spouse to abandon you is one example.

Nancy and Roger have had a marriage that could best be described as an armed camp divided against itself. Neither ever threatened leaving with the intent of carrying it out, but episodes of intense hostility from time to time seem to take the tension to the breaking point. Each time it gets worse. They are unable to sit down and discuss the nature of the problems that fester between them in any way that leads to a solution. This is because both would like to end the marriage, but both feel so guilty and so entrapped by each other's methods that they are unable to make the move and they are too angry and uncommitted to try and make the marriage work. Each is trying to get the other to leave.

Nancy is a bright girl who left drama school to get married. She resents Roger for convincing her to leave school and become a wife and mother. On the other side, she is glad she did not have to face the possibility of not making it as an actress. Part of the time she feels angry for allowing herself to get trapped in this situation; part of the time she feels angry at Roger for trapping her. Most of the time she is angry at something.

She spends every available free moment working with the local theatre, sometimes acting and sometimes directing. She is constantly having a problem with her own image; her performance never seems to come up to what she thinks it should be. Rather than deal with this for what it is—a limitation in her ability—she prefers to regard it as the result of not having enough free time because of the house and kids and Roger. The more time she spends with the theatre, the wilder the children get and the bigger their problems become in school. The children really do not get mistreated as a result of the time that Nancy spends away from the house. That is the least of it. The children have problems because they sense the mother's underlying resentment toward them for getting in her way. They rebel by being as hostile as they can be toward their own environment. Naturally, they can't concentrate and don't learn as well as they could.

Naturally, too, Nancy is so overwhelmed by her responsibilities at home that it is easy to see them as the reason why she cannot make a complete commitment to the theatre and work out some of her shortcomings. When she gives more time to the theatre and her performance still doesn't get any better because she feels guilty, her anger increases. The children get worse. Roger decides this is happening because Nancy is failing as a mother. If she spent more time at home and not at the stupid theatre, the kids would be better. Or so he frequently reminds her.

She agrees to try harder, but her trying only means that she spends more time at home. It does not mean that she is less angry. In fact, she is angrier, for now she feels doubly trapped, doubly angry. So the kids get even worse. Roger blows his stack and calls her irresponsible and a rotten mother. He begins to give her long, detailed lectures about everything she is doing wrong. He's sure he really knows what's going on. After all, he spent the last fifteen years studying her weak spots. So now he lets her have it, right in those weak spots:

"Nancy, you've got to start taking things seriously in this house. I mean it. I've about had it with all the screaming and yelling around here! You must be doing something wrong. You're not giving the kids the things they need. You should try to be a little understanding instead of getting angry at them. You know that doesn't work. You're not using your brains, Nancy. You can't treat the kids like objects. You've got to get more organized and schedule your day. You do things in such a slipshod way. I shouldn't have to spend my valuable time checking up on you. You never know what you have to do and what you've already done. If you ask me, this theatre business has really just been a bad experience for you."

"I don't recall asking you, darling."

"You have a lot at stake here, and I think that you have to fulfill your responsibilities as a mother."

"What about your responsibilities as a father?"

"What the hell is that supposed to mean?"

"Look at you! How many guys your age still don't know what they want to do?"

"You're not being fair."

"Where is a rule written that says I have to be fair? I can be just like you! Do you think you've been fair to me all these years? I had to stay home while you went out and got a Ph.D. and now you want me to stay home while you make up your mind what you're going to do with it."

"Everyone's entitled to change jobs."

"Sure they are, but every year? You haven't held a job longer than two years since we've been married. You haven't been able to get enough seniority any place you've worked to be earning the kind of salary your friends have. Look at you, the brightest guy in your class in college, everyone telling me I was such a lucky girl getting a catch like you! You were going to set the world on fire, remember? What a laugh you are! You never can be satisfied anywhere, can you? You know what you are?''

''You're going to tell me?''

''You're a flop, that's what! Whether you admit it or not, you're a failure! You've never done anything that really meant anything. And the sad part about it is that *I gave up my life* on the hope you'd amount to something.''

''Why don't you just leave?''

''Boy, you certainly give me enough reasons to!''

Whether or not Nancy leaves this time depends on how fed up she is with Roger, how much of a failure he is. Whether or not Roger leaves depends on how fed up he is with Nancy's poor housekeeping, mothering, and performance as a wife. In this situation neither is able to talk about what they really feel about themselves. The issue is always the other person. The technique is to pick the other person apart and to manage your own life so that you maximize the chance of disappointing the other. The hope is that you will drive the other out while you stay put and be proven right by default. At least to your own satisfaction.

In this situation everyone suffers. Neither gets anywhere in solving his own problems or making the other happy. The guilt over their own anger keeps them in place. Until they decide not to put all blame on the other and each accepts some of it himself, they are doomed to stay locked in deadly combat or headed for divorce. Roger must discover that although he hurts his wife by giving up his jobs so frequently, he is also afraid of confronting his own worth if he stays too long. Nancy must discover the limits of her talent and manage to live within them without finding excuses for failing.

There are other ways to get people to help you decide. One of the favorite moves of people who feel very guilty in a marriage because they are having an affair is to get the spouse to become a "partner in crime." It is an enormously childish move and a breathtaking testimony to the desperateness some people feel and their helplessness to act on it.

Beth is the person her PTA would nominate as the "Woman most unlikely to have an extramarital affair this year." It's not that she is undesirable; she is quite attractive, pleasant, and warm. The only unfaithful feeling she has allowed herself during her twenty years of marriage occurred in the wake of a pinch on the rear end she received at a cocktail party five years ago from a friend's husband who was only being playful.

Beth is a nice lady, what her friends call a home body. She is also rather unimaginative about some things; for instance, variety in making love with her husband. He feels badly about this and uses her sexual coolness as the only item he can complain about in the marriage. She views the new sexual freedom as overdone and silly. She is embarrassed by it, in other words, and still prefers to have sex in one position with the lights off and her nightgown on. Their arguments rarely get past this problem.

Her husband, George, has kept up his subscription to *Playboy* for ten years and enjoys browsing through the "adult" book stores near the office. He has read all the sex manuals, all the confessions-of-a-sordid-person kind of book that come on the market. He spends hours sitting longingly on the park bench looking at girls without bras, trying to guess just by the way they walk what sort of exotic sex they prefer. George has this intricate system, see, which he's developed over the years so he can categorize any woman in a minute. George is a nice guy although he does get a bit graphic with his language from time to time. Beth pretends that she does not hear and goes on knitting away, smiling, tolerating it all. Good old Beth, good old George!

George always wanted to get involved with someone during his marriage but could never manage to let himself go. He just wanted to experiment, he said to himself, to get a little experience with some of the things he'd been reading about. He tried a prostitute but, to his horror, he was impotent. George, the great sexual dragon killer, had been slain. George never did have a high regard for his own sexual worth. In fact, that was the reason he married Beth, because she appeared safe and nonthreatening. He knew she would never make demands on him that he couldn't fill. But now the prostitute had dragged the threat out in the open and he was forced to do something about it.

He felt wounded. Why couldn't he manage to have an erection? It puzzled him for a while. Then he decided he needed someone who really cared for him. A relationship with a strange girl was not what he wanted. George, modern man that he found himself evolving into, wanted to have an affair.

The telltale signs that every normal wife would see, pass by Beth without notice. George loses twenty-seven pounds, this time seemingly without even trying. Suddenly he is able to refuse almost any dessert, even his favorite double slice of apple pie with vanilla ice cream. Suddenly, too, all his old suits look corny to George, and he orders a new wardrobe. His old barber is replaced by a hair stylist.

"George, baby, you look like dynamite," his friends tell him. Beth thinks he looks well—well, maybe a little too sharp.

George suddenly wants to get ahead at the job and is finding that he is working harder and coming home later. It's easier, more leisurely, he explains, to schedule some clients at night instead of squeezing people in between meetings during the day. He does see an extra client now and then and more money does come in, making it all seem worthwhile and real to Beth. Beth is just content that he feels happy. She does notice that he isn't pressuring her any more in bed, but she doesn't want to question him about it. George can't stand to look at himself after a while and feels guilty. After all, his chick is not even thirty.

Now George has a new tactic:

"Beth, I saw that one."

"What are you talking about, dear?"

"I saw him."

"Who? What are you talking about?"

"Don't tell me you didn't notice that guy staring at you?"

"What guy? Really, George. No one was staring at me."

Beth is confused and sneaks a look across the cocktail lounge. Sure enough, some man looks back at her. Beth is surprised and embarrassed. What she doesn't think of is that if she were to stare across any cocktail lounge some man would always stare back. George says:

"What did I tell you?"

"Why was he looking at me?"

''Maybe he'd like to get involved with you?''

George is as subtle as a nude at a funeral, but Beth is so naive that he has to be sure she understands him. This bombardment, designed to make Beth become aware of her feelings toward other men, increases. If she doesn't have such feelings yet, George will help her discover them. At a party some days later he presses on:

''Did you notice how Bob looked at you? I know what he has on his mind.''

''Really, you think everyone just wants sex.''

''Hey, I know what a guy has on his mind. I can tell. If you don't believe me, why don't you ask him?'' Bob was the friendly soul who pinched Beth years ago. She's never forgotten it. Bob was a good pincher.

''I'm not going to do any such thing! What's the matter with you, George?''

''Hey, Bob, come over here. I want to ask you a question.''

''Sure, George. Hi, Beth. How's my favorite girl?''

''Bob, I want you to help settle an argument.''

''Please, George!'' Beth's protest is in vain. George pushes on:

''It's not difficult. Look, we've been discussing how normal it is for people to have sexual feelings about other people, whether or not they're married.''

''Sure, that's normal!'' Bob is very embarrassed.

''For anyone—right, Bob?''

''Yeah, I guess.''

''For instance, just as an example, have you ever thought what it'd be like to sleep with Sandy?'' George knows Sandy is beautiful, and he's crazy about the way she walks.

''Sandy Graham? Sure. Nice girl.''

"What about Beth?" says George, throwing Bob and Beth off guard.

"Ahmm . . . Beth? Yuh, sure. Beth, doll, when you want to get rid of this guy, call me. My number's in the book. I've got to get back, George. See you two."

"Take it easy, Bob. *(George turns to Beth.)* Well, what did I tell you? It's perfectly all right for people to have feelings like that. Bob has them for you, and I can tell you feel the same about him."

Beth is startled and does not forget the incident. Out of his own guilt, George keeps pushing his newfound morality on her and accuses her of harboring his feelings. He begins one of the greatest medical feats of the century: the complete transplant of an emotional problem. He gives Beth his guilt. Whether or not Beth talks it over with Bob, or they get further involved, is not important. George has made Beth aware of her sexual feelings and Beth feels guilty. George has set his wife up and feels better. He's no longer alone in feeling guilty.

If George finds someone he really wants to live with and wants to get divorced, he can use these ways to pressure Beth into an affair herself, giving him grounds to leave.

George is not entirely to blame. Beth's great naiveté leaves her unable to manage her husband or her marriage. She is not receptive to what is going on in her husband's mind and would prefer not to know. It may have been easy for her to act naive once, but now George won't leave her alone. If she doesn't change, she is going to get hurt.

Neither of these two rigid people want to adapt to each other. They depend on contrived events to move them, rather than discussing their feelings openly and directly. For them, any change is difficult. Even when they get back together again after an argument, nothing much is resolved because they talk mostly about external problems. The underlying conflicts in feeling and awareness are left undiscussed and so they do not move closer together. They learn nothing new except that they are susceptible to injury from a wider range of problems than they were originally aware of.

These two people are good examples of what is called a neurotic object choice. Each married someone who was the symbolic representation of what they lacked. They married someone whose personality made up for their own defects. George needed the stability of Beth; Beth needed the outgoing qualities of George. Even very small changes in behavior jar such a marriage. Other classic neurotic object choices include the compulsive, highly organized, efficient if emotionally constrained type marrying the hysterical, disorganized, emotionally volatile impulsive type. Each needs what the other provides to feel complete.

Domineering people who marry dependent people are another example. They are cemented together with a very powerful bond. So many needs are met by the other person that separation seems like losing a part of oneself. In a neurotic object choice people often choose a type more than they do an individual. The person is married because of what he stands for, not what he is. It is not uncommon for such people to see each other in a particular role with well-defined limits. When one partner outgrows his role and wishes to change, the other partner feels betrayed and abandoned.

The needs of such partners are also perceived by each other in limited ways. Each partner considers what a person in the other's role should want, rather than what the other person as a person needs. Needs that do not fall into a spouse's perception of the other person are not recognized as real needs and often go unmet. Beth can't understand George's sexual needs because they do not resemble hers. She thinks, "How could anyone want anything like that if I dislike it so much?" The two stay together in spite of not being fulfilled. Because of the strength of the forces that brought them together in the first place, and the need of each to feel complete through the other, these marriages are rarely changed by forces from within; reliance on external factors is therefore common.

Although these people seek to feel complete through the bond with the other person, they almost never achieve it. At best it is an incomplete completeness. They have reached out to another person for something they did not have inside themselves. Their commitment to the relationship is one that makes growth and personal development very difficult. As soon as a change begins to occur, the marriage becomes very unstable. Since their strength comes from the marriage, they begin to weaken and find it more difficult to make a move.

The need for external events to force a change is not restricted to marriages that are based on a neurotic object choice. In fact, in any marriage external events can force a change.

Rather than analyze the individual problems that cause conflict, people tend to let them pass by. Anger becomes swallowed. The source of the original hurt becomes more and more difficult to pinpoint and the marriage fails as if lost in a black fog. Couples begin to feel lonely when they are together and do not know how to begin to resolve their problems, because they have hidden them so long.

While this may seem to be far from the main subject of this book, it really is not. Many problems in career, profession, role, and identity are not recognized as such because they masquerade as marital problems. The problem marriage becomes the focus for many of the difficulties in each partner's personal life. The marriage takes the blame for all of the failures. It should be clear from what I have said so far that many people enter marriage because it served a need from their past. As people begin to change and their needs change, they may not wish to remain in their usual roles. The partner who is being left behind struggles desperately to keep things as they were, but unless both partners are willing to change and grow together, the marriage is severely undermined.

Frequently this becomes the setting into which the most common external event is introduced. The "other man" or the "other woman" arrives on the scene. The third party is often used to compare the partner with. Even though the third party may remain silent and not be around for long, he or she often becomes the force that helps uncover and define problems by making clear that there is a lot missing in the marriage.

There is much to insure the success of the other man or woman. First of all, third parties have at their disposal the greatest aphrodisiac ever discovered: variety. As ee cummings put it:

> and possibly i like the thrill
> of under me you quite so new

It is difficult to compete with the excitement and freshness of a relationship isolated from the old conflicts at home. The new relationship is often taken as an example of how things could be without the spouse. It is an unrealistic example. Such relationships are seductive because they often serve merely as a screen onto which the unhappy partner, seeking escape, projects his positive dreams and wishes.

People tend to fall in love with these projected fantasies and to act on them as if they are real. Since none of the old conflicts interfere with the new relationship, the unfaithful partner believes that it is possible for him to have a perfect relationship. He believes in his fantasies and has often not had enough time to test them out. He cannot tell yet if he brings problems into the new relationship that are similar to the ones he left at home. As a result of the often distorted belief that there is something much better out there, the partner now feels secure in going ahead and forcing his own marriage to the brink.

Yet some people are able to resolve many of their problems through a third person. They may be able to crystallize their view of the world through the new relationship and allow themselves to see the possibilities at home for the very first time. In these cases, the third person provides the new perspective by removing the partner from a confusing life pattern and constricting ideas.

A woman who was having an affair as a way of avoiding her own marital discords told me that she found herself doing things for her lover that she had been neglecting to do at home. She was more patient with her lover when he was in the bathroom and would never stand outside and tell him he was "hogging it all" to himself. She did not tell him that she was tired every time she felt tired. Or that her chronic back condition bothered her when it did. She did not complain about his choice in accommodations or his plans for the evening, even when she disagreed with him. She didn't think that these annoyances were important.

I asked her what the effect of that kind of indulgence toward her own husband would be. She smiled and said, "But that would be giving him what he wanted."

I suggested that the two of them had the right to be angry at each other, but that anger should be out in the open, that refusing to enjoy life as a way of expressing anger has a way of undermining all pleasure. Her ability to understand this and apply it to her marriage was the direct result of seeing her relationship with her husband more clearly through her affair.

When a partner uses an affair to prove to himself that he can get along well with another person and that the fault in the marriage is not his, then the affair will be limited by his need to keep up the appearance that everything is going well. Just as problems were not discussed in the marriage, they cannot be admitted in the affair. The admission of problems in the new relationship would be an admission of culpability in the first relationship, so the old problems are perpetuated.

It is important to determine how real a relationship with a third party is. If the third party is only a surface on to which the needs of one of the partners is projected, then the chances are that whatever results from the new union will be very much like the marriage because no real issues will have been resolved. If an extramarital relationship allows problems to be discussed and more feelings to be shared and the result is a more open way of looking at the world, it is probably real.

Besides using a third party as emotional support for the fantasies (or realities) of a partner while he forces a marriage to dissolution, a third party can also be used more directly. The outsider can be used to precipitate a crisis. This crisis is characteristically a scandal, and the "innocent" partner ends up suing for separation and divorce. Stated simply, the unfaithful partner allows his behavior to become so obvious that the other cannot ignore it, regardless of how much he or she chooses to try. Because a partner couldn't leave the marriage, he allows himself to be caught.

The paperback literature and the gossip of every card game, supermarket and hairdresser is filled with examples. It should be sufficient to say that people often get caught because they want to get caught. The only reason why a spouse finds out is because the other person wanted him or her to. Disagree with this as much as you want. I won't budge an inch. It's just the truth. If the human race handled everything with the same astuteness that it brings to extramarital affairs, we would still be trying to invent the wheel.

How on earth can a mature adult who is in possession of his senses believe that he will escape being caught? Sooner or later there is going to be some sort of reckoning. You might get away with it once, but not forever. To believe otherwise is just fooling yourself. Knowing this, people with extramarital relationships are literally asking for trouble. Specifically, they are asking for someone else to do their work for them, so they don't have to be the one to break up the marriage. Spouses who go off on very short flings do not enter this situation unless they have one going all the time. The extramarital relationship that eventually gets found out is the one where there is a great deal of emotional involvement. Even though the unfaithful party may insist that he wants the marriage to stay together—and even though he may believe this—the very nature of the commitment to the third person will eventually expose him.

Looking at it in a more critical way, unfaithful mates take chances that no sane person would, and eventually get caught. When they do, they register great surprise, and usually also great relief. Their guilt is now in the open. The flagrancy of their act unleashes an outraged sense of injury from the innocent partner who often moves vindictively and rapidly to punish the extramarital couple. In one swift move, the guilty party can now make the innocent party appear to be the heavy, by spurring him into violent retaliation. The injured party has been pushed to the point of over-reacting, with all the usual self-righteous overtones.

The new couple now feels that *they* have been injured and are being maligned. After all, all they did was dare to love each other. Kinda gets you, doesn't it? Now the tables are reversed.

The best way to act when a spouse finds himself in such a situation is not to become vindictive or outraged, but to let the couple deal with their own guilt. Too strong a re-action will just cement the ties of the new relationship against the spouse. Left alone, many of the old problems will start creeping into the new relationship. A lot of anger is really not that useful to anyone in the end.

The issues of the marriage are often not discussed in such a situation, and it is unlikely that they will be when too many angry feelings fly around. The marital partners' love for each other has been forgotten. All the old gripes are thrown into the air without the moderation of affection that makes life livable. Each partner responds to the other's recitation of complaints with a longer list. All the old skeletons are brought out.

I suspect that the reason why husbands and wives are not allowed to testify against each other in divorce proceedings is that it has all been heard before, and the problems presented by one party are more than one really needs to know. Besides, no judge alive could stand the constant exposure to the noise level that would result and trials would take too long.

There is another way of utilizing events in the external world to clarify one's own problems. Some people who find it impossible to deal with their own feelings use their friends' unhappy situations as extensions of their own difficulties. It does not matter if the friend's situation is very different from theirs; they can still project their own problems into it. The unhappy friend helps her friend "discover" her own problems—often problems that don't exist in the first place.

By giving advice, selectively reporting facts and selectively "not hearing" or observing, the "friend" manages to get the other person to make decisions that she herself would like to make. Then she observes to see how her advice turns out.

Carrie has the worst marriage in her suburb. Her husband has gone through ten mistresses in as many years. Her children all have learning difficulties. She has severe migraine headaches and has never enjoyed sexual relations. Or playing with her children or doing her wash. Nothing pleases her. Nothing except helping out her neighbor, Beverly.

Beverly's marriage has been rocky at times, but it's still in pretty decent shape and could be salvaged. Carrie has

186

become Beverly's "marriage counsellor" and over the past few months has told her to check her husband's jacket for hairs and perfume, to unscrew the mouthpiece on her extension phone and eavesdrop when he talks, to ask him serious questions in the middle of intercourse and to report back to her what happened. Then Carrie tells Beverly what it all means. Beverly is confused. With all the bad things she has discovered with Carrie's help she feels she should be much more miserable. That, according to Carrie, is exactly Beverly's problem: she should find out why she isn't more miserable! There must be something else going on!

Such a counselor is a dangerous meddler and should be avoided like the plague. People who play amateur psychiatrist try to work out their own problems through others. The offenders include everyone who sticks his nose into other people's problems, giving the piece of advice they themselves can't follow. This includes some psychiatrists, ministers, counsellors, mothers, friends, everyone. We are all guilty. Shame on all of us.

Look at it this way: if someone asks you for help, fine, tell them what you think, but also tell them why you might be prejudiced. If you have problems with your own life, there is no need to make someone else's life miserable by getting them to do what you think is right for you but are not sure about. Remember, the purpose of this book is to show you how to change and what obstacles stand in your way. It's obvious that the reason you can't change is *your* problem. Solving someone else's problem is helpful to them if you can really do it. But unless you discover something unusual about yourself while you are helping the other person out, it is very unlikely that it is going to help *you* change. In the end people solve little about their own problems when they act like Carrie, because they have risked little of their own.

And in order for meaningful change to occur, it is absolutely necessary to take some risks. Sometimes one hears reports of people undergoing sudden transformations at the hands of fate, but these are the exception rather than the rule. I suppose the old adage is right after all: "Nothing ventured, nothing gained."

Just to be certain that we understand each other, how much one must risk to initiate change is not the same for everyone. It may be a great deal for people like the business executives described in a *Wall Street Journal* article who left the corporate structure to find a way of life of their own without the usual security in their new jobs. For others it may be less disrupting—like the doctor who gives up his practice to go into research.

Taking too great a risk in the name of change and self-improvement can be a poorly disguised form of self-destruction. It is not a question of risk as much as it is of how much risk is really required, and what the motivations are of the person taking it. I tend to view as suicidal a young man with severe family and money problems who decides to go over Niagara Falls in a barrel, regardless of how much money was promised to him if he succeeded. There's a difference between reasonable risk and martyrdom.

Coming close to death is a powerful factor in influencing people to change their lives. It may be the exception to the statement that leaving the dirty work to others is a rotten thing to do, because some positive changes often result.

Dostoevski had been sentenced by the Tzar to death before the firing squad. The Tzar, being good-natured and a great kidder at heart, had no intention of *really* killing Dostoevski. He just wanted to shake him up a little and teach him a lesson to watch what he wrote and stop being so critical. As the count to load, aim, and fire was being given, a lone rider came galloping in on horseback with Dostoevski's pardon. Dostoevski did not appreciate the joke and was not himself for many months. But what he wrote of his thoughts as the horseman approached illustrates a very important point.

"What an eternity. What if I did not have to die. All eternity would be mine. Oh, then I would change every minute into a century; I would not lose a single one; I would keep track of all my instincts, and I would not spend any of them lightly."

A brush with death may be the first stroke in painting a new picture of life.

People may attribute to fate many of the insults heaped upon us by bad health when much of it is caused by our own passive neglect. If you really want to, you can make yourself much healthier than you are now, and you can stay that way by taking care of yourself and getting rid of some bad habits.

While it is not true in all cases of poor health, many people take poor care of themselves, neglect their health, and are deaf to any reasonable warning that nature gives. It is unlikely that any of them would state directly, "I am ruining my health so I don't have to do what I am doing now"; they construct their burdensome schedules and disregard their own interests to the point where they do not need to say it. Their body says it for them. It collapses.

Even when such a physical cataclysm is unpredictable, the contributing factors that lead up to it were around for a long time. You can actually kill yourself by working hard at something you hate. If that's your purpose, to die young so your survivors will be able to enjoy your insurance, good luck to you. And it is precisely luck that you'll need, because you're not helping yourself.

A heart attack at fifty is the insignia of our culture. Everyone in the family becomes swollen with grief and guilt over how hard the poor fellow worked all his life. No one was twisting his arm, if you remember. Most people who have heart attacks have been under pressure and did not succeed in moving away from it. The only nice thing about having a heart attack, assuming you survive, is that you absorb the full impact of how little you really contribute that is irreplaceable. Others take your place in a hurry.

You're worried, you say, because you fear you will not be able to work again? That's what the nurse relates to your doctor as he makes morning rounds: "And Mr. Green feels he will not be able to work again, doctor."

"Nonsense, Mr. Green, I looked over your EKG and it is really coming along. The ST segments look great! You look better. The sed rate is normal again and the other blood tests are getting back to normal. Damn lucky, I say. You've had a warning. You've got to change the way you live."

The doctor failed to respond to the patient's signal that (besides dying) this man fears that his contribution to his job is unremarkable, totally replaceable, and that he is really worthless. Mr. Green feels an even greater pressure to hustle back to the job and break his neck to prove how much he is worth. What he should learn is that very little of the time and effort he expends are really essential; that he could be more selective and concentrate on the things he does best, things he is suited for; and that he'll then produce a great deal more work with much less effort and very little pressure—just because he likes doing it. Instead, when he leaves the hospital, Mr. Green will probably try to prove to his colleagues that he can do all of his job and theirs as well. Better reserve a bed. This guy is going to extend that injury and maybe even kill himself. In fact, many cardiac patients begin to have pain again the very day they are told they can leave the hospital.

How do you write and fill a prescription for a new way of life? That's what Mr. Green really needs, and that's what this book is all about.

We all kill ourselves a little when we take on jobs that lie beyond our particular area of expertise. We work under strain and generally perform poorly. By doing the things that we like best, we return control of our lives to ourselves. We become less concerned with ''getting ahead'' and begin to enjoy the moment. When we do what we are suited for, we are most likely to succeed and to live to enjoy our success.

When Zinka Milanov, the great soprano, was asked why her voice had lasted three decades with little appreciable change, even though she maintained a strenuous schedule, she replied that she only took roles ideally suited to the range and quality of her voice. She refused to strain or force it. Instead, she developed it into one of the world's most magnificent instruments. You may say that she could afford to pick and choose, but this is not so, for she made the choice at the beginning of her career. Her singing appeared effortless throughout the decades.

All of us can usually pick and choose more than we admit.

Further blockbusters that fate thrusts upon us include the loss of loved ones, war, natural disaster, and other forms of going broke. In going broke, you sometimes find that since you have nothing, it is just as well to start something else. One cannot lose more. It is only when large numbers of people go broke together, and there are no examples of others' success to borrow hope from, that a depression mentally begins to set in.

Last I should mention the role that the passage of time plays in people's lives. There are several big birthdays that may act as external "stop" or "start" signs. Thirty is the end of youth and is generally regarded as the time for having a last fling, the time for making changes. As I have mentioned before, the birthdays that follow are not much different although everyone who turns forty or fifty would disagree. They only heighten the feelings of desperateness. In a real sense, birthdays are really death days.

In sum, people do a remarkable variety of things to get external factors to change their lives. Usually, this method is slipshod, unpredictable, and too diffuse to help much. There is a better way, a way that puts you in control of your own destiny.

10

MAKING YOUR OWN DECISIONS

The only one way to make a change in your life that will have the maximum chance of success is to examine who you are, what you think you need, what you would really like, what is really possible—and then to come to a decision about it by yourself. If you are looking for a simple answer in this book, you are really looking for some external force to tell you what to do, and you've come to the wrong place. All I can do is point out possible pitfalls, common mistakes and what they mean—the common patterns and what they hide and a method for moving out of them. That in itself is a pretty tall order.

At this point you should have learned much about human resistance to change and should have discovered why people act guilty; how they put the blame on others; what fears they have; the cultural forces affecting people and how these forces operate; the roles that people play; and how people rely on external events. If you want to get more out of life by doing a great deal less than you are now doing, and are sick and tired of not feeling good about the life you lead, you need a new direction.

We have looked long and hard into the way things are and how they got that way. What we need to know now is the answer to the simplest question of all. What are you really looking for? I mean, what do you want out of life? Put it another way: years from now, when you are lying on your death bed, staring at a ceiling that is growing dim, what regrets will you then have for not doing something now? Just think how unimportant all your excuses for not doing what you want will appear then. Look back at your life from the vantage point of that death bed, feeling yourself grow cold and distant. It's not pleasant to think of death, but that is the only perspective from which you can realistically think of life. Inside you a little voice is calling to you. What does it say you should have done? *What does it say?*

No one knows the answer but you, and for me to fill this page with images to lure you is not what you need. This book is no trick, no seduction by an outside force. It is an attempt to help you look at what you want. For example: What have you envied in others? Did you envy them because you didn't have what they had or because you didn't develop their skills? Anyone can have a fur coat. But what about a smile? Do you envy someone's smile of self-satisfaction or of completeness or sureness in knowing they have chosen their own way?

Every decision about the contents of your life is related, in some way, to the question of emotional freedom. How free you *are* depends on how much you have come to terms with the external forces in your life and with the pressures from inside. An external force may demand that you succeed. An internal force may demand that you resolve old feelings such as pleasing your father. I have tried to show

how both forces can throw you off your private, special track.

Are you off on another wild goose chase? Are you just an escapist, running away from the pressures of reality to find momentary comfort in some hideaway that has little to do with reality?

Artists confront themselves more than anyone else in our culture, and artists' colonies are rarely hideaways that exclude reality. They are enclaves that contain whatever part of the world these people have decided to work on. To them they are the world. It is the outside that seems unreal. Who is to say they are wrong? The artist in a work retreat is not usually hiding from his artistic self. How can society call him an escapist for confronting himself? Some people question whether the artist's life is any way to live. Should self-expression be one's major consideration? Ask the artist with whom he would change places. Would he change places with you?

As a matter of fact, who *would* change places with you? How much could you get auctioning off your way of life? Who is jealous of your life, the things you have done? Is *anyone* you respect jealous of what you have done? Bear in mind that people without children are bound to envy your children and people with fewer material things will be jealous that you have more. But who is jealous of you because of what you are? If the answer to that is, "No one," including yourself, then you certainly have some thinking to do about making your life special and full. But to run away without thinking is just escaping.

Escapists are easy to identify. They usually run when they are in some kind of crisis. Although they run far and fast, they have made no real decision except about where they don't want to be right now. They are not running *to* somewhere. They are running *from* something. Even when these people claim to be running toward something, this is soon unmasked as an escape, because they will run to the next place just as quickly when problems start creeping up on them again. Everyone tries to escape sometimes, and wanting to escape doesn't mean very much. It is an urge, not a solution. Leaving to get a better perspective and intending to return is not an escape!

It is very common during a marital crisis to want to leave for a new love, thinking that the old one is gone and irretrievable. People who say they have never felt this are either not being honest or are not very self-aware. These feelings allow introspection in a marriage and permit real growth to take place. People who say they have never felt this may have missed opportunities for growth and may be living in a doll's house where everyone is committed to remain as they always were—to being unreal.

There is no sure guide to tell whether a new love is real; no more than there is a sure way to tell whether an old one is dead. You must always be cautious about the risk of falling in love with love—comparing someone with whom you have had a long-standing relationship to a fantasied ideal, a creature who lives only in your daydreams. It is enormously destructive to go through marriage hating the spouse for not being someone else—for not being what they cannot be. The other only learns to resent this (even if it is never expressed) and finds it more difficult to give of himself. When a person is constantly compared to a standard he can never meet, and always found lacking, he feels undermined and seldom secure or able to give or to love on his own terms. Since such a person expects failure, he stops trying.

Isn't it better to accept him for what he is? If your needs are such that you cannot accept your spouse without comparing him to an ideal person you feel you need, or if you cannot be with the spouse without measuring his shortcomings, and if you honestly believe that the two of you are incompatible, then perhaps it is time for a change.

Certainly, if your spouse truly cannot change (which is rarely the case), he is entitled to be loved by someone for being the way he is. And, do you know, somewhere out in the world there *is* someone who can love him just the way he is, who can accept the shortcomings that you can not, who can appreciate things you don't even notice. What right have you to hold on to someone only to curse the dark side of his personality? What about the side you never see? Perhaps you may not find what you need in your marriage, but you should not punish another person because your needs are difficult to meet. Especially when someone else can give them the appreciation and love that you can not. If you cannot love someone for the way he is, the chances are that the feeling is mutual.

Although it may be difficult for some to admit, people do not change their basic personality very much during their lifetimes. We all know people who seem to disprove this, but if one looks closely at them one finds that the traits which now seem so different were present when the person was younger; they just were not expressed. If people seem to change personality, it is only that they allow different aspects of it to show through. They do not become a different person. Their *attitudes* change.

Even a slight shift in personality traits may seem drastic,

but it is really a rearrangement of a person's priorities. Because of a new perspective, those attitudes and goals that were terribly important before are no longer so important, and one is now free to move on. Most of us are freer to move on than we realize, but have held back out of habit. We have grown accustomed to the compromises we made with ourselves. We have put away the dreams that once crept into our consciousness and have dismissed them as ridiculous. Question: if they are ridiculous, why do they keep coming back?

Although you can alter the way you look at your own life and personality, it is infinitely more difficult to change personality. A psychoanalyst, one of my supervisors during my psychiatric residency, once discussed with me the feasibility of personality change through extended psychoanalysis. He said: "If you analyze a bastard, after seven years you end up with an analyzed bastard, but he's still a bastard."

I do not take such a dim view of the prospect of change. I feel that people can alter their lives very significantly—the way they feel about themselves and the people around them—even if they do not change their basic personality very much. It is a matter of doing the best with what you have.

In order for this to happen, it is necessary that the person with whom you spend your life can love the good points about you without continually demanding that you make changes to fit their preconceived expectations of what you should be like. This demand only creates anger and encourages rigid ways of dealing with each other; this precludes growth and diminishes one's chances to be happy. In such a situation one is not appreciated and loved for what one is and the spouse is always disappointed because his expectations are not met.

Before making a decision, look at your life and its contents and consider whether you are perhaps fooling yourself by planning a change. Do you already have most of what you really want if you can learn to accept yourself more, including the fact that you may not be as clever or as talented as you'd like? What you are, you are. There is a danger of rejecting the outside world because you cannot live with yourself.

A very real possibility exists that you can do a great deal more with your life right where you are if you begin to do more with yourself. If you are not as good a writer as you would like to be and have put off writing that novel, why not take some courses in creative writing? You will need the courage to face your shortcomings, but you cannot polish up your skills until you know what needs polishing. I've already discussed many of the common fears that represent ways people use to avoid looking at shortcomings they'd like to overcome. It is essential that you examine your assets and liabilities, personality quirks and peculiarities and decide to what extent you get in your own way; then you can take this into account and adjust for it. We all get in our own way to some extent. And to some extent we all would like to avoid facing up to it. It seems so much easier to make a change first and to wait until conditions improve before we look at ourselves. But if we do this we are only running away. Such a new venture will probably fail in time, even though the situation may look better in the beginning, because the real source of our failure was us to begin with. That problem must be looked at first.

Everyone gets bored from time to time, but if you have been bored for a long time, you must ask yourself whether you are just looking for thrills if you're thinking of making a drastic change. What is wrong with just seeking to find a more pleasurable way of life? What's wrong with moving to a Spanish fishing village and living off your savings for a few years, reading books, talking to people over a glass of wine in the summer sun? What's wrong with that? Is there anything wrong with taking time out to enjoy life and to think?

There's nothing wrong with it if it is the fulfillment of a wish rather than a way of avoiding problems. After all, taking time out is what people are supposed to be doing when they retire. It is acceptable as a reward at the end of a life of hard work. Why should it be wrong to seek it now?

Look at it this way. If you tried to train a dog but only allowed him to smell the doggy treats you keep in your pocket, and you never gave him any to eat when he performs correctly, the dog would not stay interested.

How is it possible for human beings to stay interested in their work and life with very short, rushed, cramped vacations once a year, if they bother to take them at all, and to postpone what they want for years? Why can't it be possible to shape a way of life that is its own reward? Why do you have to postpone moving to a warmer climate where you can swim all year until you are so old that you're afraid of the water?

The leisurely life provides great dividends in terms of new perspective and understanding to the person who adopts it when he is still vital. Sometimes he returns to his former surroundings with new energies and direction and succeeds where before he did not. Leisurely contemplation has been ritualized by many societies and assigned to specialists. The convent represents the establishment side of the contemplative life in our society. On the other side, the hippie communes go in for very much the same sort of activities: shared fellowship, a search for the transcendental experience. The hippie commune also utilizes the sensual and sexual approaches to the mystical experience. This is simply because these communal societies are heterosexual. Sex plays a part in all monastic life, whether its influence comes through the enjoyment of the sexual experience or from repressing the desire and trying to master it. The difference between the groups is not great. All monastic groups have used drugs. It is only the drugs that change and the rituals concerning their use. The older the religion, the more symbolic and less sensory is the use of the drug. The wine at communion is not consumed to give a "high" but to share a symbol. Smoking hashish at a commune may inspire a new sense of community through a shared way of perceiving. The religious community perceives the same vision, the commune using drugs shares the same process of perceiving. Both feel alike.

Monastic groups were allowed to break away from society and establish a new order away from it and with fewer responsibilities than people in the workaday world. Like the wealthy and landed who were trapped by their own social standards even though they had other license, monastic communities had other restrictions. The departure of monastic groups from society served as the symbol for everyone leaving society. The others worked, the monks contemplated for them. In Japan, monks still contemplate and retreat for weeks trying to solve some community problem which the pressure of daily life seems to prevent the villagers from solving. One man in one small community enters the contemplative life so society may function. In order that the departure of one man does not destroy society, his departure is only a ritual. He never physically leaves.

What is wrong with our society that we cannot take part in the contemplative life, the life of self-assessment? In order to make any kind of major decisions about one's own life and its meaning, it is necessary to spend much time by oneself, to think things over. But there are very few corners to run to. It seems as if almost no one is taking the time to find out who they really are. Most of us are too busy being busy, never stopping to figure out what really counts in life.

If you want to make a decision and you want that decision to be the right one, going away for a while, alone, with no one to bother you, may be one of the best things you can do. The process of freeing oneself from surrounding problems takes concentration and seldom happens in a few days, but it is worth the effort. It is worth the start. It is also sometimes valuable to discuss feelings with strangers and get new bearings on life. To try to work out problems within the old framework and patterns only makes it more difficult. A new view is needed, free of old prejudices.

What do I want? What do I have? Have I anything to gain? Should I stay where I am? Am I really happy doing what I want? How can things be changed? These key questions must be looked at over and over again. The answers are never easy. Very few people in this country really know much about thinking a problem through in a contemplative way, allowing the mind to run wherever it wants and examining afterward the feelings and images one has seen.

This passive state takes time to induce. The best method of solving problems is not always active or predictable. The answer you will finally reach is not likely to be one that you already know and need only pick from a few other possibilities. The new answer for you is part of a personal revelation, a personal self-discovery that takes time, persistence and thinking about.

If you are lucky and begin to examine your life today, to question what you believe, the values you live by, whether or not you are getting enough out of work, your home, the way you live, it will probably take you the better part of a year to implement a decision. Any decision that comes quickly should be suspected. It may be a substitute that will lead to further disappointment and entrapment later.

Fortunately, the "final" decision is not final at all. It is more of a tentative step, well-planned and launched under conditions as favorable as possible to insure success. The idea that things are going to happen quickly is naive. People want a great deal, and it is possible for them to have it, but it is necessary that the process of change be slow and orderly. Events may progress faster than one can imagine, if things go smoothly and the early successes are encouraging. Unlike other investments, the investment of more in one's self as things look better and better actually tends to reduce the risk and insures success in the end.

Be as realistic as possible. You cannot have the moon. In fact, you probably don't want the moon or even many things you have been vaguely wishing for. More likely, what you really want is something you find difficult to define exactly, at least at the moment; this arises because it's difficult to accept that there is so much you do not now have.

If you feel you are trapped in a spiral of materialistic acquisition, it becomes difficult to say just what you really want. All you can say is that you want a lot. If you are miserable with yourself and project your dissatisfaction onto the world around you, nothing will seem to give you pleasure; the answer to the problem remains within you.

You have lost your focus on yourself. The only time things appear in sharp focus is when you look at an immediate goal: your pay, completing the ironing, sitting down with a drink. These short term goals seem very important, but they have no lasting effect to make you content. Yet they seem so clear. The goals to make you happy are not on the same focal plane as the short term goals. No matter how clearly the day-to-day things in your life appear, their satisfactions are fleeting. You must lose your focus of the everyday world, look behind it for a new set of images and begin to zero in on them.

External and internal realities must be examined in making a major life change. The external reality is deceiving because it will appear to change during the period of examination and contemplation, seeming at one moment to be the worst possible situation and at the next to be too good to leave. The external reality is always changing between two vague extremes. It may vary daily. External reality should be judged by its flow from one extreme to the other, not by focusing on any single point exclusively. Reality is based on all the points in the experience. The reality of our day-to-day life is that some days it is good, some days it is bad. We are trying to find how reality *usually* is. This must be appreciated in order to deal with the possibility of a major change to another set of realities that will also offer constantly changing conditions.

We must decide what the new reality is usually like. The danger is to judge the reality of the new circumstances by one of its extremes.

Many things that you accept in the outside world as reasons why you should stay or leave really aren't what you think they are, at least not most of the time. Confusing? Not really. The boss whom you thought to be cruel and holding you back turns out to be just a boss. *You* were the one holding yourself back. The husband you felt was rigid and restrictive about you taking a job turns out in the end to be fairly sympathetic to the idea. It was your abrupt way of presenting your wishes that seemed to turn him off originally. And if you remember, you were relieved when he objected, even though you were angry. It was not till you came to terms with yourself that you could present the idea in a way your husband could accept. And, incidentally, in a way that had some chance of succeeding.

You must attain a new perspective for viewing the contents of your world in order to be free from the prejudices that made it impossible to deduce anything but the old conclusions.

Reality, then, is a collection of experiences that can be rearranged by prejudice, fear, or ambition. Actually, reality is what we make it to be. The world is a collection of objects and feelings held together by concepts. The concepts change from culture to culture; and what is accepted as reality in one culture often does not make sense in another. Honor, duty, responsibility differ vastly from culture to culture.

We call something unrealistic when it does not seem to take the facts into logical consideration. We have enough facts in our lives. What we need is a new way of forming concepts about them. We need a new reality, a life expressing a greater truth about ourselves.

The process of making a decision is the process of becoming a reasonably detached observer to the events in the world around you. The parade of events that fill your day must be looked at from time to time as if they were unrolling in front of you on a screen.

The managing of the house and your role in it must be looked at anew. Look at that person you think is you. What is that person doing and why? How does she feel when she feeds the baby? When the baby is sleeping? When she is talking on the telephone? How does she feel when she is cooking? What is she thinking? Who is she thinking of? What does it mean? What does she want now? What would she like to do now? What does she feel about other people who are doing things and feeling things? These questions must be asked over and over until new answers begin to appear, until new questions and new conflicts begin to come to the surface. Answers are really not what you need most. What you need more are the right questions. Such as: Is this enough for me? Should I be doing something else? Is there another world I would like more?

Every aspect of one's life and routine is worthy of examination to see if it can provide the crack in our self-protective armor through which we can see a glint of light. No one is so rigidly entrenched in a system that he will not be able to find a new way of seeing himself if he takes enough time and repeats the process. If you slowly, persistently watch the images of the day pass by and experience the sounds, the words in the air, you will begin to see things anew.

One must try to experience the world in a new context. You must use your senses as if you were discovering them for the first time. Too often our senses have become bogged down in preconceived prejudices. We expect the world to be a certain way, and somehow that's the way we experience it. To begin to experience the world differently you must change the way you perceive it. To show how much you have been missing in life, to get an idea of how much is happening around you without your knowing it, to understand that you make decisions out of habit or based on a few superficial appearances, try the following experiment.

Take a record of some piece of music that you know quite well and listen only to the lowest instruments in the orchestra, never letting your attention drift to the higher instruments. You will become aware of an entirely different way of hearing the music. Next, extend this experiment and look at some paintings by focusing on specific lines or colors.

A marvelous experience is to watch television for an evening with the sound turned down. You see more.

A day can be spent focusing on different smells.

The whole idea is to expand your awareness of sensory impressions. As I will show, this is useful because it lets you develop concepts about you and your life. If you are aware of more about you and the world around you, your ideas about yourself will change.

This is a way of thinking and being that is unfortunately alien to most people in our culture. Many of you reading this may think that it's crazy. Why should you find answers to anything by just sitting and becoming passive for a part of each day and looking at the world you are living in? Who is writing this? Some eastern fakir?

It is true that contemplation and distance are used in many eastern religions. That is not what I refer to here. I intend for you to use passivity and the passive state (which is not to be confused with the passive positions many people take because they do not want to appear aggressive) but to use this approach in a creative way.

The creative process can be very useful in helping people make discoveries about themselves. While working with creative people over the years, I have developed some insights into that process that could be very useful here.

The artist, when creating, engages in what I call transitional thinking, a form of thought that has been preserved to a greater or lesser extent in all of us. What we do with it depends on taste, skill and training. We all have access to it and can learn to use it more.

Transitional thinking first becomes evident in an infant who is learning to tell the difference between his own body and the rest of the world, between his thoughts and what he perceives outside of himself. The infant cannot tell whether he sees something or whether he is only remembering it. As a result, one often observes that babies, after screaming for their bottle for some time, begin to make sucking motions while waiting for it. They soon stop sucking and appear to be full. When it arrives, they refuse the real bottle. What happened? The infant "remembered" the old bottle, and since it cannot tell thought from reality, it accepted its mental image as real and was satisfied by it.

This sounds incredible and far-fetched, but it is a generally accepted concept.

The infant begins to see the world as a collection of objects and feelings that at first are not attached to any meaning or prejudice but do become meaningful to him as his experience grows. He learns to do whatever produces pleasurable feelings and to avoid whatever creates pain. This is called the Pleasure Principle. Eventually he learns to postpone his need for self-gratification and pleasure. This postponement is the beginning of socialization; its goal is not the eradication of the infant's drive for pleasure; rather, it's the enhancement of pleasure by making the infant wait until gratification can be most appropriately accomplished.

Somehow that goal—pleasure—becomes lost in our culture; too many forces compete to make us postpone our wishes.

Besides placing objects and people into the categories of pleasurable or painful, the infant's view of the world is remarkable in another way. The infant sees the world *without knowing* that he is seeing the world. He just sees, hears, experiences. In his attempt to arrange that chaotic group of sensory impressions into some system that allows him to find pleasure, he begins the process of creating order: creating concepts about things and forming ideas about them. All these ideas are new to the infant. He moves back and forth in this *transitional* state from a world of chaos to a world in which there is some order.

The artist is able to engage in the same kind of thinking. He is able to remove many of the symbolic meanings that are usually attached to ideas and objects and to think about the world without using words to define what he experiences. The artist watches a parade of sensory images passing by. Words appear like sounds. Objects appear as colors and shapes. After a while in this dreamlike state without words, everything begins to appear chaotic—just as in the infant's world. The artist then tries to impose some new meaning or form on the disorganization he has just perceived. Like the baby, he regards his new order as real. This attempt to reorganize the pieces of the world constitutes the heart of the creative process. It is a new order, the beginning of a new reality.

Employing this same kind of thinking may permit new ideas to come to the surface, especially new ideas about who one is and what one's life means. Our old ties to the objects and ideas and values of our world interfere with thinking about things in a new way. Trying to imitate the creative artist in thinking about solving problems may prove quite helpful.

Look at it this way: if the way you usually think about things is so effective, why are you still stuck in the same old rut?

We tend to think that an attitude is good because we have been taught that it is good. We accept things as being worthwhile mainly because we have always accepted them as worthwhile. When we think about things the way the creative artist does, we are able to remove some of our prejudices about how things are supposed to be. Like the infant, we become aware of two distinctions: is something pleasurable or is it painful?

When we return to this basic way of appreciating objects, people, and ideas in our life, we may find it easier to make decisions about them. It is sometimes surprising to return home after a long absence and have Mother serve what used to be your favorite meal, only to find that it is not as good as you remember it. The usual response is to think that the old girl has lost her touch. But what has probably happened is that you have changed your perception and conception of Mom. When you were younger, mother filled more needs for you, and the nourishment that her food provided satisfied more than hunger. The distance you now have from Mom and your other sources of emotional supplies will now allow you to appreciate the food more for its taste than what it stands for.

We need to develop this kind of distance in viewing other things in our lives, all of which I have mentioned before. Then we can see how they really taste to us. We love Mom, but we no longer need all the things that she once provided. We can provide for ourselves on our own now. In fact, we could destroy our identity if we moved home. We have gotten used to a different diet; the wonderful care we once received would be a ferocious pain in the neck if we had to put up with it.

While it may seem ridiculous on the surface to extend the analogy this far, many links to people's goals are based on the fact that they have never moved out of their home emotionally. They don't belong there and they feel miserable, substituting bosses and routines for their parents. It's time they grew up. Their needs have changed. Just because something once produced pleasure doesn't mean that it still does. Some things once thought to be disagreeable may now be capable of giving great pleasure.

When children are told about sexual behavior for the first time, one of their most common responses is, "Not my parents! I would never do a thing like that." We can see that attitudes change when the drive is strong enough. We must adapt to the new reality of the world that we perceive

211

and learn to enjoy life for what it means to us. Obtaining distance is the first step in finding out what it really means.

One of the questions to be answered by getting distance is whether or not you really want a new life or whether it is possible just to change your attitude and get new pleasure as a result. Much of your success will depend on your attitude; it must be liberated from the forces of the past that constrict it. This liberation happens gradually as you understand the strength and direction of your wishes and needs.

There is much you cannot run away from and that you must deal with. And it is time that you begin to see yourself honestly as a person with feelings who is easily hurt, who is vulnerable, who often feels lonely and sometimes unfulfilled. This is the reality of the human condition, but not its ultimate destiny. No one can learn to accept what he merely pretends he does not need. The acceptance of these needs is a prerequisite to fulfilling them, no matter how painful and how alone this admission makes one feel.

It is not possible to run away from your inner truth, whether you are in contact with it and free to speak about it or not. Feelings of self-doubt, self-hatred, insecurity, shame, guilt and pettiness are part of all of us and determine what makes us happy. These feelings indicate that more is needed. To deny them is to increase the isolation from ourselves and make fulfillment less possible.

During the process of making the important decisions, you will begin to see more of yourself than ever before. At first this will come in fragments, little snatches of the truth that you catch. You must begin to take a step backward every so often into that special world of the observer, the world of the artist creating.

To become an observer of yourself, it is useful to try to

sit in a quiet room, close your eyes and think of nothing for five or ten minutes. You may feel totally ridiculous trying it, but think of it this way: all you can lose is a few minutes. After a few days, increase the time to twenty minutes. You can open your eyes if you want; it's really not that important.

You should *not* use words to think. Just look at objects. Don't think about looking at them. Just look. Don't make decisions or judgments about the beauty or ugliness of what you see or even think of the names of things. That is not what all this is about. What you are trying to do is to observe things in the light of the way they appear, without reference to your past experience, in order to put them together in a new way. So you must not use words because words have meanings that will restrict the way you see what you are looking at.

Try this while looking out the window at people. When you get good at this technique after a month or so, you will be able to turn on this kind of thinking whenever you want.

If you have a specific problem, it is useful to think about the problem for a brief moment and then return to this wordless kind of thinking, just allowing the sensory impressions of the world around you to flow by. Somehow, just thinking of the problem briefly will direct the process of thinking toward it.

This process clears the mental apparatus of its old prejudices and allows thoughts to occur without words and without their symbolic and defensive inhibitions. After a while you may discover that you are able to come up with new ideas and will not even know where they came from.

The way this happens is not entirely clear, but probably resembles the way an artist creates. When the usual meanings are removed from objects, a state of disorder results; things are seen without reference to how they are used. They are not grouped together in categories as they usually are. Instead, they are perceived as having a shape, a color, a texture, a temperature, a reflection. They are reduced to a collection of sensory characteristics. An apple, for instance, is shiny, round, cool, red, smooth.

When a person resumes thinking about things using words, associations are made between the similar sensory characteristics that were seen in different objects. The old way of experiencing is changed. Many sensory aspects of objects appear that were not even noticed before. It is possible to make connections between objects and ideas that were impossible before. When one begins to reorder the world after experiencing this self-induced disorganization, it is possible to put things in new categories and make new decisions.

I can imagine you thinking, "How do you like that: in order to change, I have to go into a trance!" Never mind. What you are looking for is a method of dealing with the facts of your life so that you can come up with a new solution that is right for you. The right answer depends on the way you feel about yourself, not the way you think you should feel about yourself; on the way things really are, not the way you wish they were. The retreat into this non-prejudicial fantasy where you observe yourself is one way that will help you find the way. You begin to change by beginning to think again.

How can you tell whether a decision is right for you? At this point you should know that this is a matter of time and constant re-examination. There is no easy way. There never was. The trouble is that you have spent so much time making up rules to live your life by—and avoiding pleasure—that it is hard for you to break them.

Another way of saying this is that the way for telling whether your decision is right or wrong is not yet available to you. How you finally judge what you have done, or decide what to do, will depend on forces inside you. You do not now and you may not ever completely understand them. You must allow these feelings to express themselves and you must deal with them before you make a decision. Even if you don't understand them, you must accept them and acknowledge their existence.

I am aware that this may sound like avoiding the question and seem far afield from offering constructive ideas. If you had the ability to make a decision after all the facts in your life were pointed out, you would not have any problem to begin with. However, you *are* aware of the different problems in your life and much of what you feel about them. What you are not aware of are the other possibilities outside of your usual way of seeing things, beyond the grip that the past has on you.

To take charge of the present requires that you give up some of your old ways of structuring the world. You must learn to see the world anew, perhaps for the first time. This takes time and a great effort. The alternative is never to change, never to know, to ponder the growing darkness about you and feel cheated and alone, to die isolated from yourself, unfulfilled.

The decision will be right when you are right for the decision.

11

WHAT IF YOU'RE NOT GOOD AT ANYTHING SPECIAL?

Many people reading this are probably asking, "What can I do about all this? I don't have any special talent or special ability. I really don't even have a special interest. All I know is that I'm dissatisfied with what I'm doing and the way I'm living. I don't even know what to begin to think about."

Being dissatisfied is reason enough for wanting to change the way life is going for you. After all, you only get one chance to live. Why not live fully? The fact that life seems unrewarding to you indicates you have needs that are not being met. So, how do you determine what your particular needs are?

Some things everyone needs because they are necessary for basic survival: affection, shelter, food and clothing. Not much can be gained by discussing these; you already know all about them. The needs that are not so obvious differ from person to person. They define who you are and that, in turn, is a reflection of the way you were brought up.

These needs are often more difficult to identify because they are really another way of describing who you are.

What follows may seem silly to some readers and may not be taken seriously. But if you have little idea what you want to do, it may prove quite useful. It may also be useful if you think you do know, because it provides an additional perspective.

Think about the events in life that have made you happiest and put them down on paper so that you have a list in the order you think of each item. This will give you an inventory of what pleases you. This may sound silly, but if you try it, you may be surprised, even if it is only at the order things come to your mind. The order in which you put them down may tell you quite a bit about yourself. If there is something you like very much at the bottom of the list and something you like a lot less at the top, you can see how much your sense of duty and obligation have interfered with getting what you want. You should put down on paper as many satisfactions as you can possibly think of, even if you have to stretch your imagination. I urge you to do this now, before you read any further.

On another piece of paper make a list of all the famous people, living or dead, whom you admire most and put down two qualities that you like best about each one of them.

Next, make a list on a third piece of paper of those events in your life that you wish had never happened. Write down the name of the feeling you felt about each individual event, such as embarrassment, hurt, envy, guilt.

Now make a list of everything you wished for most as a child and whatever you wish for most in your adult life.

Finally, put down the most frequent compliments you receive.

Now go over each list individually and try to put each item into a category, such as material, financial, family, personal achievement, social. Look at the category where the largest number of items fall. This is the area of your greatest interest. While no specific ideas may be staring you in the face, you should begin to see some pattern, even if it is merely a repetition of the rut you see yourself trapped in. It is easy for you to be trapped, for many people have so restricted their world that they do little beyond their routine activities to fulfill themselves.

But there is a way out.

Examine the items in the "personal achievement" category on the first list and see if you can notice anything particular about yourself. Are the events similar? Do they point to a common interest?

Do the same with the other categories; compare them. Do you see preferences appearing that you already know about? Or do you see some surprises?

Try to group the qualities that you liked about the ten most famous people into categories: personal achievement, family, social, material. Does the category that represented your greatest interest appear often in the people you admire? Do the same qualities repeat? The qualities you admire in others may not appear to have any relationship to those you find in yourself. This is because what we admire in others is often a reflection of how we wish we were. Compare the lists with this in mind.

Are there any similarities between this list and the first list you completed? If there aren't, then the list of events you disliked may provide a clue to your feelings, because it will show where you are most sensitive to hurt. Try to see what it was that you reacted to in each case.

Finally, take a look at the list of wishes you made and divide that into categories. Then look over everything you have worked up. What you have done is compare your wishes with reality. Now you should see a direction or field that holds an interest for you.

Let's take a look at a set of lists prepared by a suburban housewife who, in spite of being very active, felt that she had no real goals in life and was getting bored spending so much time at home. She had waited for the day when all her children would be old enough to be in school. Then, she hoped, she would feel free. To her surprise, she found that when that time finally arrived after her 38th birthday, she did not know what to do with herself. No matter what she did, she still felt incomplete.

Here are her lists:

LIST 1 (Happiest memories)
1. Having a husband and a family I can love (family)
2. Having a nice home (material)
3. Leaving my parents' house (personal)
4. Finally not having anyone in diapers! ! ! ! (personal)
5. Husband's promotion and raise (family)
6. Running charity ball last year (personal)
7. Finding out I wasn't pregnant last year! (personal)
8. Planning Jerry's wedding (personal-social)
9. Shopping (personal)

This list of this wife's happiest events indicates a person who is concerned with being independent and free of household obligations, especially taking care of very young children. She enjoys organizing and planning social events.

Her family and home have given her pleasure, but she still needs more to make her happy.

LIST 2 (Most admired people)
1. Jackie Kennedy, social esteem, glamorous (social)
2. Mrs. Henry Ford, always giving parties (social)
3. Mrs. Lyndon Johnson, social graciousness (social)
4. Paul Newman, handsome (personal)
5. President Kennedy, his comfortableness with the people (personal)

This list shows a strong interest in becoming someone who is involved in social activities and meeting people.

LIST 3 (Unpleasant memories)
1. Nearly drowned when I was six (personal) (terror)
2. Dog was run over (family-personal) (hurt)
3. Injury to my eye (personal) (fear)
4. Being stood up for senior prom (social) (embarrassment)
5. Grandfather's death (personal) (hurt)
6. Not having a chance to have a career (personal) (hurt)

This list will always include some losses.

LIST 4 (Wishes)
1. A nice home (material)
2. A nice family (family)
3. To have a great husband (family-personal)
4. To be liked (personal)
5. To make something of myself (personal)
6. To have a very busy and glamorous social life (social)
7. To have money (material)

This list is very similar to the first one, the happiest events in her life. Since her wishes appear to be fulfilled, one would expect her to be happy now. All the desired ingredients for her happiness appear to be there. But since she isn't happy, perhaps she isn't putting her life together in the right way.

LIST 5 (personal compliments)
1. Good housekeeper and mother (family)
2. Give great parties (social)
3. Great cook (family)
4. Have good taste (social)
5. Know how to do things the right way (social)

This list indicates not merely what she gets compliments for, but also the compliments she remembers best, the ones she is most pleased to receive. Again, we see a person who would do well in a social setting.

This woman has an unusually strong interest in social activities. Unfortunately, the limiting factors in social involvement are money and family status, and these may be difficult to change. If this woman looks at her wish to be involved in social events in terms of joining "high society," she will feel frustrated. But she also has an interest in taking charge of social affairs, i.e., planning weddings and running the charity ball. Her friends see in her the ability to know what to do socially and how to organize social events. The people she admires also have strong social interests. The disliked events in her life are rather typical except that she still remembers being stood up at a prom as being very important to her. This woman is sensitive to being rejected. She has a strong need for personal growth and to be independent.

Looking at the total picture, it is reasonable to suggest that she look into the possibility of opening up an exclusive party consultant business to plan and organize affairs for social groups or charities. It seems to me a natural interest for her. She would meet the people she wants and win their esteem by doing what she already knows she does well. There is always a market for a skill that you do well. The trouble with most people is that they do not know that their skills are worth anything because they come to them so naturally that they take them for granted. This woman could also give courses in an adult education program on how to give a party or other related aspects of home entertaining. It would be easy for her.

What would be easy for you?

It is impossible to tell anyone what to like or what to do. The only way you can find out is to look at satisfactions that mean the most to you and, if necessary, to try to find some others that are similar but more attainable. Many kinds of tests try to identify one's interests in life, but these tests are approximate and not as valuable as looking into what has already given you pleasure and avoiding what you know to be distasteful.

Don't throw your lists away for a while. Look at them every so often over a period of a few weeks. Then ask yourself whether there is anything you would rather be doing than what you are doing now. If you were able to have any three wishes, what would you pick? Write down your choices and go over all the lists again to see if you can tell what things are truly important to you.

By this time you may have developed some idea of what you would like to do. You may actually have known it beforehand but were too afraid to say it, even to yourself, because it seems so difficult and so unlikely to be fulfilled.

If you still have no idea of what you want, it is likely that you are the sort of person who either doesn't do a great deal of thinking about himself or who gets trapped over and over again in old thoughts. If none of these suggestions has produced any ideas or led you to consider something new that might interest you, it might be that you need some new experience, some new inputs so you have something to contrast your life with.

A good place to start to look is right where you are. Most people do not know what is going on in their own community. Dozens, sometimes literally hundreds of events happen daily in every major city that could interest you if you give them a chance. It can be exciting to try something new that you've not done before. We all run the risk of not growing by saying "no" to things before we even know what they are really all about. There are always new skills to acquire, a sport to master, a craft to learn. There is something, somewhere, worth trying, even if one has tried before and regardless of the previous results.

You should look merely for the purpose of initiating the process of looking. If you've tried something and it doesn't please you, try something else. Many goals are found by accident while looking for something quite different.

The answer is not in learning something like a new hobby just to have a hobby; that in itself can become busy-work. You should try to experience the feeling of doing something just because you like it and perhaps to become skilled at expressing your feelings in a fresh new way. Maybe you do not have enough talent to become independent solely by pursuing a new extracurricular activity on an extended basis. That is not the question. If that new endeavor makes you feel better about yourself, if it gives you a clearer perspective or increases your control over something and helps you establish your self-confidence, it is valuable. It is valuable just to feel special.

There is no magic, no short cut and no secret way of discovering what you like and what you would do well to become. That is a matter of trial and error. Look at it this way: if you don't try to get yourself out of the rut you are in, who do you think will?

If you expect a book to give you the drive to conquer the world, you're wrong.

People who find that the world holds little for them are usually waiting for something to happen to them. They usually wait a long time. Don't be that way. What people find to be special in the world is often what they find to be special in themselves. Just as we project our own fears onto the world when we are unsure of ourselves and need excuses to justify our failure, we find we can learn to project our hopefulness onto the world and discover reasons for taking risks and succeeding. Opportunity is often attitude.

Maybe after you follow through on these suggestions you still feel that you are not particularly good at anything or that you just don't have any talent, anything to make you feel special. You are almost certainly wrong, although no one really knows for sure. Do remember that it is bound to take a long time to discover what ability you do have. What we call talent is the skillful expression of a feeling in some medium, using a particular style. Success depends on feelings, skills, native gifts and hard work. The native gift is a very small portion of the entire effort. The skillful expression of feelings takes time to master. The ability to express feelings in some symbolic form other than conversation is possible for all of us. As for talent, everyone has some ability to do something if one looks for it. The trick is to find it and to stick with it. That is where the hard work comes in.

The greatest potential for changes in a person's life does not depend on his talent but rather upon his attitude toward himself. One does not need to find an art form or craft in order to be free and creative and happy. What you want is probably closer to you right now than you think.

Shelly became depressed after her last child graduated from college and left home. Shelly had always been a good mother, but had never seen motherhood as her sole purpose in life. Neither did she see a special meaning in anything else. She had been her husband's pleasant confidant during the rough years and now when they were comfortable, she was needed less by everyone. She began to make depressing visits to her friends. Actually, they were condolence calls in reverse, because she was the one going around looking for sympathy. Shelly became the world's biggest pain in the neck.

"Shelly," said her closest friend, "you've become the prophet of doom around the neighborhood. Why don't you go to the club?"

"I've been to the club."

"Then go for a drive."

"I did. I drove over here, didn't I?"

"Where did you get the dress you have on? It's stunning."

"A little designer I know in New York."

"And the shoes?"

"I know a man in Philadelphia. I flew down."

"Shelly, is your coat new?"

"I had Georges LaRoux do it."

"Don't know him."

"He used to be with Givenchey."

"You know *all* these people. Did you put it all together yourself? I mean, how do you do it?"

"I don't know really. Over the years I've come to know all these designers. I certainly have bought enough clothes in my life to support all of them."

"Well, you always look perfect!"

"Thanks, but that doesn't help. What am I going to do? I just sit around all day and feel like tearing the wallpaper to shreds."

"If it weren't so crazy, I'd tell you to open a boutique."

"That *is* crazy!"

"You could call all those designer friends and have them supply you with the things you like. You helped a lot of people choose their wardrobes. You really have."

"A lot of people do ask my advice."

"Shelly, this *is* a great idea. You can open up a little shop and send announcements to everyone you know in town. You're not in it to make a fortune, so your prices can be reasonable."

"Do you think it would work?"

"Why not?"

"I don't know anything about business."

"I do. I'd love to help out. I can manage a store. You do the buying, I'll do the selling."

Does this sound very unrealistic to you? Or would it be so unusual for someone to begin to market their homemade food specialties locally? If you have ever been told, "No one makes this like you," then you have a business to go into. What you may be missing in your search to find something to do could be right in front of you—something for which you already have a great deal of skill. Perhaps decorating or being an instructor in homemaking to disadvantaged people, or being a big brother or big sister to a child who needs guidance because he is minus one parent.

There are activities that you do well, that you take for granted because they come to you so easily. *Those* are the very things to look at closely. Those are the talents you will be able to develop quickly and most easily. You may need the help of another person along the way, but don't let that stop you. You'll find the person you need in time, because news of what you are doing will get around and people with similar interests attract each other.

If you believe that your job or role is the only one you can do, you are probably wrong. There is almost certainly something else you can do better and more easily. If you look at yourself closely, there is something you now take for granted that may be the key to a new career you would enjoy. Hey, it's all right even if you think others will call it silly. If you like doing something, do it.

Observe the people you see each day and ask, "Would I like doing that? Could I do it?" There's nothing wrong about working with your hands. There's nothing wrong with anything you really want to do or be. It's your life to lead.

I know two men who own a large construction firm. Both are millionaires. While they do all of the administrative work in the company themselves, they like more than anything else to get out with twelve-pound sledgehammers and break down walls and crash through windows and make a great deal of noise and mess. They thoroughly enjoy driving a bulldozer into a building and razing it. Although they have been successful for years, they wouldn't give up the physical aspects of their work for anyone. They love it. They are under little pressure, even though they work very hard physically. In their close contact with their work, they have been able to increase their earnings by discovering more efficient ways of tearing down buildings.

They enjoy getting up early in the morning and working hard all day. If they had allowed their company to grow larger, they would have had more administrative responsibilities. They decided that they had more money than they could ever need and agreed to keep their enterprise small and manageable. As a result, they are more efficient and more successful than they could have been had they expanded, because they are in control. They pay special attention to every detail and oversee each project. They can charge more for their efforts, because their quality is better. What is more, because they are on the job all the time, their losses due to theft and waste are minimal.

In this country we have lost much of this acceptance of things that are small and manageable. The pressure to enlarge is enormous. When people give in to it, they often lose control of themselves and then are unable to find what they can relate to or identify with. Sometimes one gets bigger by getting smaller.

Ideally, one should try to express one's traits and personality in work. To run a business or produce a product that contains part of your own personality is something that other people may or may not appreciate. You run the risk that people may reject you because they don't like your taste or style. You can't please everyone. Some disappointment is bound to occur, but to be accepted at something because of what you are is gratifying, and to accept oneself is peace.

Most people have worked so hard at smoothing rough edges off their personalities in order to "fit in" that there is little left of the original flavor that made them unique; little that they do that someone else could not do as well. What is worse, there is less and less that they can call their own. True, they are able to fit in now, but like the square peg that has been cut to fit a round hole, the fit is imperfect and much has been lost. A perfectly good square peg has been made into an obviously faulty round peg.

The *Wall Street Journal* recently carried an article about the president of IBM issuing a memo discouraging all employees from wearing bright colored shirts. The expression of individual taste is related to creativity. Demanding that the employees conform to rigid dress standards will result in their feeling more constrained, angry, and less willing to work. The president of IBM obviously does not understand what motivates people to develop their fullest potential. Even in this small way he runs the risk, through limiting people's self-expression, of decreasing the inventiveness of his company. People have enough difficulty being creative without this kind of hindrance. The pioneering spirit that made IBM the great innovative company that it is would have been crushed by an attitude like this. It was the different color of IBM's shirt that made it so special years ago.

Any new idea is going to upset someone. We've seen that, but that's no reason for holding back. An idea that cannot be expressed in one company will find its way into another. Such pressure to conform eventually pushes out the most innovative people, and unless this attitude stops,

IBM will become a company where its employees are so concerned about conforming that they cannot help the company grow. I wonder what would happen if the IBM wall plaque that reads "THINK" were replaced by one that says "SELF CONTROL"?

You can see how much harder it is these days to go against the system. The foolish things we allow to control our lives often have as much sense behind them as the president of IBM's memo. Sometimes, although it's hard to believe, they have less.

One thing you do better than anyone else in the world is to be you. That may sound trite and totally uninspiring, but it also contains the truth about what you can do best. You must decide what it is that makes you, you. Part of who you are was reflected in the lists you made at the beginning of the chapter. There is some special feature of you, of your being, of the way you interact with people, that makes you different. It is something you do not *try* to do. It is something you *are*. It is there just as sure as you are.

What is it? What do you think people appreciate most about you? What is different about the way you see the world? It's worth looking into.

You may still not feel you are good at anything special, but that does not mean you cannot be. There is some place where your specialness can shine. Somewhere that difference can be expressed. It's up to you to find it, and you can.

If you begin to look for this in yourself and then try to find a way to realize a life that allows you to do what you want, your life will become better for you than you ever expected. People who have been accepted because of some particular part of their personality begin to feel differently about themselves. They become more in control, more willing to change and grow because they feel more complete as a person. To say that you have no special talent and no special ability is to state only that you have not looked hard and widely enough, that you haven't been seriously enough interested to really try. There's no need to hide from yourself. You'll find something, even if it doesn't meet all your wishes.

Why put such a great effort into doing things the way you do now—only to feel dissatisfied? And it's not a matter of how much you try to do that makes you happy. It's *what* you try to do. There isn't anyone, anywhere, who could not, by looking more honestly at what makes him unique, find something, some field of activity, some ability, that would allow him to struggle less and get a great deal more out of life. When you think about it, it's ridiculous not to try living the way you want.

12

BREAKING AWAY
AT LAST

Any change you make entails problems, but when the change involves a new way of life or living, the complications can seem endless. People who you once thought were your friends start to tell you morbid stories of failure—it's as if they wanted to wish you bad luck. (Do they feel anxious about going out and challenging themselves?) And you're sure to find your own problems, too, along the way in search of yourself.

Let's face it: if you're really determined to make the big change, you may be making the biggest mistake of your life. Just think of it. You've probably upset your entire household just by deciding to look at yourself. You have openly admitted that many of the things you've been doing have been a waste of time and no real challenge to anyone with brains. You've offended people like yourself by rejecting their way of life for another that you believe to be better. You've announced your intentions and you're ready to shove off.

You may indeed be wrong. You may really be making a mess out of your life. Anyhow, those are the doubts that cross your mind over and over again as you stand watching the movers take out the piano, your favorite chair, and the boxes of books and dishes. How could you ever come back to all these people and listen to all those "I told you so's?" It would be unbearable. This has got to work! All the plans! You are almost positive that you're right, that you have made the correct choice. Then why are you sitting there practically immobile, wracked with doubts?

Just look at how difficult it was to make the decision in the first place. The pros and cons that you sifted through for months. The way you considered all the effects of this upon others. You considered everything and decided to change because changing seemed the best plan. But why are you trembling? Don't you have faith in yourself? What's wrong?

Well, every question you decided had a "yes" and a "no" side to it before you decided. You did look at both sides and at yourself in the light of how you really felt. You picked one side over the other. The facts behind each decision remain the same. Only your attitude to those facts is different. Since bad things do not fade away like shadows in front of a rising sun, the negative sides of those questions are still there and will still give you some doubts from time to time. If you don't feel doubts, you probably are only fooling yourself, or perhaps you didn't take enough time to look at both sides.

As soon as anything goes wrong, the old doubts will start to reappear. This is not because they are truer than before, but because you feel your case against them is weakened by new evidence. Negative feelings, like positive ones, are always looking for support. They jump on any misfortune and use it as a wedge to pry open their case again.

The real problem is: it's hard to live with the fact that there is a negative side to every point and that it will not disappear by wishing it away. Such wishing is very unrealistic and can only undermine your plans. Denying negative feelings in order to prevent them from coming to the surface takes a great deal of effort and may limit your ability to enjoy what is good, what you changed for. If you deny so much, your new situation, in spite of all its promise and hope, will eventually become as dull as the situation you left. The only way to avoid this is to accept your negative feelings about your decision as part of the way life is and not to expect miracles. Then you can cope with them.

The decision you made was based on the reasonable expectation that the new way would probably be better. But surely you never thought life would be perfect or that the old way was entirely worthless. If you saw it that way, you wouldn't have had any problem making the decision to change. As a matter of fact, it would be very unlikely that you would have been where you were in the first place.

Let's not kid ourselves. You still need (and depend on) a lot about the situation that you left. To deny this is to deny your needs and to make it difficult to find replacements in the new situation. You still need security, though not as much as you thought. You still need friends, though you don't want a social calendar that commits all your time and robs your energy. It's not that your needs have changed as much as your attitude toward them has. You still need many of the same supplies. It's just that you want them on your terms now. You are less willing to earn a living just to earn a living, to keep house just to keep house. You want it to mean something.

Your new situation may hold a lot that you need. It may allow you to grow and discover real happiness. But before this happens, you must be honest in accepting the good and bad of both situations. The problems that you do not want to see are there just the same. You know the path has a few stones on it. Don't travel in the dark.

The very worst thing you can do is to pretend that you have no more doubts, that you are one hundred per cent sure of yourself. You may be some day, but it is unlikely that you feel that way now. Only people who have so many doubts that they cannot deal with them must take this attitude. To pretend to be completely sure is only to set yourself up for considerable disappointment and hurt.

Contrary to popular belief, you *can* take it with you. You can bring all your old unsolved problems with you and not even be aware of it for some time. The people who are most susceptible to this are those who tend to discover the reasons for their failures in the external world. To themselves, they are never the ones having problems; it's always someone else, who they often feel has it in for them. We all act this way from time to time. It's part of the way we protect our self-esteem when it's threatened. No one really likes to accept responsibility for his own failure. No one likes to feel that he has screwed things up. Clarinetists blame their reeds when they squeak. Surgeons complain that anesthesiologists aren't relaxing their patients enough to allow them to work well. Women say the butcher gave them tough meat. It's easier to blame others for our own mistakes.

People who tend to find excuses for their shortcomings will probably find similar excuses wherever they go. The names of the players may change, but their roles and the basic game will remain the same. Before troubles can get better, the excuse-maker's attitude must change.

Barry owns a grocery store in a very rough part of town. He dislikes the people who come into his store and spends hours complaining about them, how they steal from him and try to cheat him, that they're all miserable bastards. But, he adds proudly, they don't fool him; they don't get away with a thing. We all know people like Barry. Sometimes they just appear bigoted and crude. Sometimes they seem weird, but usually they are neither. If you talk to them they appear pleasant in other ways, but their ability to function seems to depend on blaming others. About this they seem rigid and unreasonably picked upon. Barry actually likes several of his customers as individuals, but for the most part he hates them. When Barry talks about his life he sees them as the reason for all his misery:

"After all, you know what kind of people these people are. You give them an inch and they'll rob you out of house and home. Do they have any respect for a man's work or what you do? Nah. Do they have any respect for a man's place of business? What do they know, they're all ignorant. They're animals. They come into the store and act tough and try to threaten me. They don't know how many of them I've helped out. How many times I've given things to them, knowing I'll get nothing in return. Do they appreciate it? Nah."

"Why do you do it, Barry?" asked one of his friends.

"I don't know. I guess I'm just a good-natured slob at heart. Maybe I'm just stupid. If I hadn't stayed there in that store, I could have done a lot. I wanted to move out to the suburbs and open a gourmet shop, but I stayed there."

"Why'd you stay?"

"Every day I keep asking myself, 'Why am I staying here in this dump?' I don't know why. They don't appreciate it. I keep the food fresh. I don't try to pass off old food like some of these others do. I'm honest. I don't charge more on payday either. I don't know, I don't know why I stay."

Barry almost seems to like the system he built for himself. He never needs to take the blame for his own failure to get ahead. He can always find someone to unload the blame on. He can go around feeling sorry for himself and even a little proud of his self-sacrifice.

After a series of fires and hold-ups, Barry moves from his ghetto store to a gourmet shop in the suburbs. The best clientele. His old dream comes true.

"You must love it, Barry," said the old friend.

"Why should I love it? Do you know what a rough time these people give me? Can you believe how much time I waste? Today I had to help some lady find the exact kind of imported preserves that she had last year in Norway! No matter what, they're never pleased. They talk down their noses at me as if they're better than I. They think I don't notice. We all came over on the same boat, you know. I'm no different than they are. I can tell what's going on behind their smug smiles. You think I don't know about these rich old society ladies making brownies with marijuana in them? Who the hell do they think they're kidding? I waste so much time with their stupid complaints that I never get my work done."

"Why don't you leave it?"

It is unlikely that Barry will ever feel free anywhere from the pressure of other people giving him a rough time because Barry is stuck in his rut thinking. If he leaves his work or changes his occupation, he will bring his style with him. There will always be an angry crowd making life difficult for him.

While the pattern that Barry creates for himself and then totes along with him is easy to detect, other people's ways are more subtle but equally painful. They also are hard to abandon and are usually packed right along in the suitcase with a person's shirts as he plans to change. These problems are characterological, problems in one's pattern of adapting to life and other people. Most of us try to react to others in a way that takes into consideration the subtle variety of human variation from one person to another. We try to see people as individuals, each with his own story to tell. When people are seen as stereotypes, they evoke stereotyped reactions. The possibilities for variation and adapting become fewer. Experience becomes blunted and life loses much of its sparkle. Our self-perception becomes the way we see the world. We respond more to the world inside us than to the world without and we bring ourselves with us wherever we go.

People who react in this stereotyped way react with what are called derivative feelings. If a police officer always produces a feeling of rage in a person, it is safe to assume that the person is not reacting to the police officer but to what the officer has come to represent. The feelings are derived from something that is going on inside the person, not from what is happening in the environment. The person who reacts this way is not really affected by the other person in a human way. He is not touched by the human experience of sharing. What the person with derivative feelings reacts to may have little to do with what is real.

When these difficult people do make a change, they chronically find themselves in similar situations as before. This is predictable because they take along the only environment that means anything to them, the one inside them. Barry is an extreme case, of course, but we all do it in some small way.

Each of us has a distinct way of dealing with situations. It's our own style of feeling and acting. It remains pretty much the same, no matter where we go or what we do. Even though your life and work patterns may be less malignant and easier to endure than some mentioned here, they do create problems.

People who are dependent on others will continue to be so in a new environment. People who become passive in the face of hostility will remain so in the future. The same is true for people who respond to stress with psychosomatic illness or by becoming rigid or compulsive, depressed or anxious. All will continue to show their characteristic life-feeling pattern. To expect this to change merely by moving one's situation is unrealistic. As long as a person is aware of his own style, he can make allowances for it, adapt successfully and avoid situations that tend to bring out his worst points.

We can alter the way we respond. First we can change situations so that the new one does not overwhelm us with stress and force us to rely on stereotyped responses merely to exist. In a less stressful situation we are freer to interact and to let responses come more individually.

People tend to get defensive when they are in threatening situations. We rationalize, intellectualize and deny our inadequacies. Some people like Barry use the entire way they react, their "style" of living and feeling, as their defense.

People who use their life style as their defense tend to become rigid. They are like the pathologically suspicious person or the person who is always uncontrollably angry. Even these people do better when tension is decreased. Then they feel less threatened and may become more flexible in their response. If Barry were in a situation with fewer demands on him and less contact with people, he would begin to feel more in control.

We can also learn to adapt to reality in new ways. We can learn to give up some of our stereotypes and change the style of feeling we normally depend on, after we realize that the old pattern does not work and why. Old beliefs about ourselves can be altered and new ones developed. Psychotherapy tries to accomplish this through a trusting relationship that investigates the sources of feelings and actions, allowing one to give up old, ineffective behavior.

However, psychotherapy accounts for only a small number of the major changes that occur in people. Any relationship between two people that is characterized by trust and mutuality can be the source of the strength needed to change. Under the pressure of great external stress, external reality may seem more important than one's own feelings. This is why so many people choose to endure stress rather than face themselves.

Everybody has known somebody who became successful and whose personality appeared to change, frequently for the better. The new position of strength sometimes makes it possible to give up self-defeating behavior. To leave an unpleasant situation for one you really like may be very helpful in allowing you to begin a new phase of emotional growth.

For better or for worse, whatever problems you have,

they are not going to stay as they are. If the pressure in your present situation decreases, they may improve. More likely you will be the same person with the same problems, but because of the decrease in stress and frustration, you may feel and appear better.

If you do change and something goes wrong in the new situation, don't get too upset if the old problems seem to recur. If the new situation is right for you, the problems will probably improve as you start making gains.

If you have hurt someone's feelings in making your move, you are bound to feel some guilt from time to time. Some of this guilt may result from your seeing your action in part as an angry act toward the people and surroundings that held you back for so long. If you managed to get someone else to play the role of the heavy, you might feel guilty about this. Everyone feels guilty when they set someone else up to do their dirty work for them (see Chapter Nine).

Sometimes following a long overdue decision people feel guilty just because the change feels so right. Imagine a young man who has left medical school to continue his earlier studies as a concert pianist. At first, he is overjoyed and throws himself into his work. At last he is able to do what he wants. In the back of his mind are thoughts of how disappointed his parents are and how much they sacrificed for him to become a doctor. The way his exuberance and completeness contrasts with his parents' feelings is enough to make him feel guilty. If he gives in and does not continue in music to avoid disappointing others and to avoid feeling guilty, the stage is set for much more serious trouble. It will surely follow as resentment (over being denied) grows to the boiling point.

Some plans are destined to be difficult to put over. It is important to be able to recognize these problems when they appear. They often have as their basis the proof of a person's worth, like Lowell trying to be as good a lawyer as his father, rather than the fulfillment of a dream. Here the person is not free to act the way he wants. Rather, he is reacting like a child running away from home to "show them." The people to whom he is reacting are so important that it is very difficult to make decisions in his best interest. In adolescence we learn that maturity means being able to do what we want *even* if our parents happen to agree with us. The person who reacts only *against* the will of others is not free to that extent. He is ruled by the other person, not himself. Often he is not sure why he does things. If such a person plans to make a change and discovers his action is approved by the very person he was reacting against, he finds it difficult to follow. If he does follow that direction, he is doubly damned. If he is successful, he pleases the person he was reacting against, and so he loses. If he fails at what he is doing, he does not get what he wants and so he also loses.

To be one's own agent means that you are free to do whatever you want, regardless of what others think. Then at least you fail or win for yourself and can enjoy the results when they are favorable.

In general, plans designed to prove something to others, rather than to fulfill oneself, go poorly. They tend to get out of hand. Since another's approval is the goal, it is literally outside of the person who is doing the changing. As the goal is approached, the response of the person to be spited is often found lacking—if indeed the target notices at all. Larger goals are then undertaken in an attempt to get a better response, and this is just as unlikely to be successful. Success, when it does happen, will not be very fulfilling. Goals that are directed at fulfilling you are concerned with a smaller segment of the world—your own world, not somebody else's. The fulfilling goal is in large part the opportunity to do what one wants. For example, when one paints for oneself, it is important just to be painting. When one is trying to prove something, the act of painting gives little joy. The picture that results must meet someone else's approval. When one paints for oneself, one need only enjoy what one is doing.

Even when a person does something solely for his own enjoyment the time will come when, as his skills and expectations grow, the results of the work begin to take on increased importance. But, unlike work done mainly out of spite, the work itself remains fulfilling. Choices made in reaction to other people have less of a personal investment behind them. They tend to remain constricted and often do not show real growth. They are inhibited by guilt. Lowell, the lawyer, could not progress to a higher position because of this.

In fact, when a choice has been made in great anger against another person, the guilt that often results may express itself as self-defeat. Some people are very difficult to be angry with.

Ann had been a good writer in college and had taught school for a few years before she married. Finding herself less than satisfied at home by the few hours a week she spent writing, she got a job with the local newspaper and used the money to pay for help to take care of the house and children and to finance a month for herself at a writers' colony. Her husband, who had not been consulted previously because Ann felt he would become furious and uncontrollable if he found out, became furious and uncontrollable when he did find out. He demanded that she quit. He claimed she was making the wrong move at the wrong time and was being impulsive. Besides, he needed her moral support because things were getting difficult for him in his business. Ann argued that she would be better able to help him if she felt more secure about herself.

Ann could not convince him and would not give in. After a few weeks at the writers' colony and after a barrage of letters and phone calls from her husband, each reporting that the house was falling apart and the children were lonely, Ann found it impossible to work effectively. She believed in her heart that she was right, but her anger at her husband grew and grew. Because she had placed herself in the role of the person leaving the home to find herself, it was difficult for her to be angry and awkward for her to express it. Everyone else in her house had already signed up for the role of the injured person and there was a waiting line of furious complainants.

Ann's anger began to intrude on her thinking and soon she could not write at all. She had begun to take out her anger on herself. She gave up the struggle and returned home, mumbling self-deprecatory statements about her lack of talent and her opinion that she never had a real chance of making it as a writer.

This scene is enacted in many families and with many varying scripts, but the basic problem is the lack of real communication between the two partners over many years prior to Ann's departure; a lack of mutual understanding; and the failure of each partner to wish for the continued emotional growth and fulfillment of the other. Some spouses feel so threatened that neither is allowed to grow without feeling that he is taking away from the other.

In spite of these problems, the gains you will make when you finally decide to make the right kind of change will well outweigh the negative points. This chapter is not intended to make you say "no" to your feelings, but to allow you to say "yes" with the best possible chance of succeeding. Without knowing what most people stumble over, you run the risk of tripping over your own feet.

13

WHAT IF IT DOESN'T WORK?

Sooner or later, if you stay at your new adventure long enough, you are bound to fail. This is not said as a threat to put you off, but to point out something everyone likes to ignore. If not expected and taken into account, it can undermine your spirit and destroy everything you have taken a risk for.

Some points to remember: first, you have not been living your new life for very long and are probably involved in activities that aren't fully familiar to you as yet. Secondly, the ways of measuring your progress may not be as clear cut as they used to be. If you were employed before and now are your own boss, you may not earn a regular salary and may be seeing less money coming in than ever before. There is an excessive tendency in our society to measure success by money, but the things you do to earn your living should have a value in themselves. After all, that's why you made a change. So you should avoid calling the change a failure just because there may be less cash rolling in.

Next, it's important to remember that in the beginning of a new activity there is always much room for improvement. You are probably still in some phase of growth. Your accomplishments may not be as great as those of others you meet who have been at it much longer. But the feeling you get from improving and seeing a chance should be as important to you as the final results. You should be able to visualize a day in the future when you will be able to function the way you expect. Almost every week should seem to bring that time closer. In other words, the weeks in your life should become a series of steps toward your goal. You should be looking at time as a friend working in your favor, not as a villain, rushing you off the face of the earth.

Still, there will be moments when you are going to feel the hurt of failing. You may discover that you have run out of money and need to take a temporary job to finance your dream. Even though you may have failed in the short term, you still know the satisfaction of having tried. It is a good feeling to fall back on. And if, for the time being, you do return to a work or life style that's not part of your dream, at least you know why you are doing it and you will know when to leave. You are not trapped forever. You know *that* situation too well. But the fact that you have failed on the first or second try will be upsetting. Don't let it make you give up. And don't let the fear of failing keep you from trying.

When upsetting reversals occur, it is important that you keep such developments as much as possible within your trusted circle of friends. Remember all the people who sat on the airstrip shouting, "It'll never get off the ground"? You don't want to waste your energy shouting back, "Yeah, but it did fly for a short while." You will be able to say "It's flying, look!" if you just keep your mouth shut and try again. Also, why put yourself in a position where you feel you have to prove yourself to anyone? That's unnecessary. What if your new situation finally is a failure, after all, and you later want to quit? Why should you feel doubly defeated because you told people that you would be able to set it all straight?

People who work at anything involving individual creativity, in general, and in the arts in particular, often fail at what they do. This is a natural by-product of the creative process, not proof of their limited ability. The process of creation is almost as much a process of selection and judgment and taste as it is the ability to produce in the first place. One or two good lines buried in an otherwise horrible poem are unable to save the poem and make it good. In fact, the bad lines appear even more horrible by contrast with the good. In this way the creative person's excellent efforts almost seem to go against him, bearing witness against the less inspired things he does.

People who are just beginning to tackle creative problems—such as finding themselves—do not have the experience of those who have been creating for years and are likewise subject to disappointment, disillusionment, and depression when they fail in their creative attempts. But the veterans have one important advantage: they've become used to it.

Sometimes one's effort just doesn't work. It is not good. What does this failure mean? To the person who has been producing every day for years, it means only that the particular attempt doesn't work and should either be thrown out or extensively revised. It just doesn't work. That's *all* there is to it. Perhaps the next one will be better. Bad results are bound to happen now and then. The law of averages says so.

When someone who has only been working creatively for a short time produces bad results, he feels that the time left to him to pursue his new creativity is limited and may feel a desperate need to succeed. This is natural because he was in the wrong area most of his life. So suddenly he has pangs of self-doubt. He thinks, "What did I do wrong? There must be something wrong with me that I have to correct. Maybe I need more training, more study or more apprenticeship? Maybe I should give up because, well, just look what happened! Do you expect me to believe that the person who did that had any natural talent, let alone skill?"

A beginner's creative failures are often taken as proof of his flimsy worth. Nothing could be more unjust.

When the experienced person says "It didn't work" the novice says "I did a terrible job." All anyone can do is start again. The worst you can do is fail. So what?

Fear of failure is ingrained in many people. They lack energy and courage to try to learn from failure, to overcome it by creating something new. Understandably, the same fear that makes people postpone and delay before they give up their old way of life often gets in their way again when they try to master their skills. But hear this: if you could get up the courage to begin, you have the courage to succeed.

Not all inspirations are noble or worthwhile. Fewer still are great or universal. The best one can do is to make an attempt to create and stay with it. Sometimes long periods of worthless production do occur. In all likelihood, these represent nothing more than clearing out the cobwebs so that better creations can occur. And without old strings attached.

First novels are a good example of this sort of thing. They are, almost without exception, self-conscious, auto-biographical, emotionally cathartic, and usually their style is highly influenced by other authors and *their* own hopes of who *they* will become. By definition, such first productions cannot be great, although there are exceptions. The exceptions often turn out to be not the author's first novel, but the outgrowth of several previous unsuccessful, unpublished failures that have never seen the light of day. This process of failure causes a certain amount of junk to be produced, but this is a necessary preliminary to something better.

The person who embarks on a creative life and is not prepared to throw out everything he does and start again is really not going to last very long at it. You might as well face it now: trying and failing are the routines of creativity.

The same can be said for almost any other new undertaking that involves giving expression to your own feelings and realizing who you are. If you are not prepared to fail, you may be overwhelmed. During the years when you kept yourself from doing what you always wanted, you may have lost your perspective of who you are and what you can do. Before you made the decision to change, you may have felt that you could do well at a new life even though you had had no real exposure to it. You may have set yourself up for a big fall because untested dreams have a tendency to grow out of proportion.

Much of what you attempt to do in your first few tries, be they in a new business, a new career, a first job, a change of environment, will be to express at once all the ideas and thoughts you have held back. The logistics of cramming all these ideas into one first attempt are quite difficult, and the first try may end in failure. However, it is likely to be a failure that makes everything ultimately possible. If you plan well, you may avoid future failures.

To fail is a natural consequence of trying. To succeed takes time and prolonged effort in the face of unfriendly odds. To think that it will be any other way, no matter what you do, is to invite yourself to be hurt and to limit your enthusiasm for trying again.

At times perhaps success does seem impossible, and you may feel as if you will never know what it is to fulfill your dream. The time for trying may be wrong. The time for succeeding may be wrong. During certain periods in a person's life nothing seems to go well, no matter what. During some periods, no outward expression of energy appears to yield movement forward. That's the way life sometimes works: in cycles. People who rely on their individual productivity all their lives usually manage to arrange their lives so that when the drive to succeed is present they can respond to it by being totally available. When there is no inspiration, they become involved in the technical work that processes the material they have created.

It is probably a good thing that there are non-creative periods, although I know of very few creative people who enjoy these spells. It is so much easier to work on the swell of a creative push than at any other time, even though it may be exhausting and perhaps even take over one's entire life for a while. But the re-working required to make an inspiration successful can be done when you're not caught up in the spirit of creating. Success, in fact, depends on these times.

William Butler Yeats, the great poet, had long periods when he was unable to work; one lasted as long as two years. Rossini stopped composing for several decades. The spirit comes and goes and the flood of energy and self-confidence that it brings is evanescent. You must take it when it comes and go wherever it leads you.

Even if you do fail, you cannot, yes, cannot fail completely. Even if you do return to the very thing you left when you changed (Would you ever allow yourself to return to the same old routine? I doubt it.) you will be reassured by the knowledge that you tried, that you had the courage at one point to face yourself and follow what you believed in. Too few people muster that courage. But those who try are never the same again. They have a new knowledge about themselves. They are closer to the truth, even if that truth is knowing that they cannot have everything they want. They have not lost their hope. They have found a larger part of themselves and have grown in the process. They can dream again and try once more.

The worst thing one can do is not to try, to be aware of what one wants and not give in to it, to spend years in silent hurt wondering if something could have materialized—and never knowing. People who have impossible dreams that they never test—and would not be able to fulfill even if they had the chance—do not know themselves. They are not able to take their shortcomings into consideration or make new, more realistic plans that they can manage and succeed in. They never learn that many lifelong wishes are unrealistic. Only those who struggle to find themselves discover that fact and alter their dreams to find something at which they finally feel successful, finally self-fulfilled.

In the end, the only people who fail are those who do not try.

14

SOME ADVICE FOR PEOPLE WHOSE SPOUSE IS PLANNING A CHANGE

What do you do if you find that your spouse is considering making a major life change? For this discussion let's assume that the change in the offing is not a divorce. What to do in the face of a divorce is a very complicated matter indeed. It could be the subject of a book in its own right. Let's assume that your spouse wants to change but wants to stay married to you.

If your spouse is about to change, you are most likely to become anxious and feel threatened. There are several reasons for this. You may feel that you are not able to make the necessary adjustments in your life to meet such a challenge. You may feel that you are going to lose many of the satisfactions you have worked for, including things you considered goals of your own over the years.

One of the most serious threats is the possibility that your spouse has outgrown you. If the person who is seeking change is the woman, the man often also feels sexually threatened. The worst thing you can do if you feel that your spouse has started to leap ahead of you is to act helpless and make him feel guilty, as if he is abandoning you. The chances are that, if given half a chance, he will be helpful and try to make your transition from the old to the new as smooth as possible.

After many years of bickering and threatening to leave his job or his wife, Howard, a disenchanted draftsman, decided to take up landscape architecture. His new interest seemed the first genuine enthusiasm in years. His wife recognized something different, something sincere in this wish. At his coaxing, she began to take an interest in flowers and they worked in planning and designing together. Many of the old tensions disappeared and they were able to make a second start, not merely in career, but in a higher level of truth in the marriage.

The threat of losing the spouse may become overwhelming. Newspapers are filled with reports of divorces that followed a success on the part of one member of the couple. But success rarely does this to people as a matter of course. The key is that success allows people to see themselves differently. It allows them to act from a position of strength and sometimes to admit to failings that they previously found impossible to concede. It is in the light of these new strengths and insights that the marriage is now weighed. This same honesty is expected of the partner who is not planning a change. The partner who wants to change wants to look at the marriage anew. Attempting to hold on out of fear, to cling to the old ways, could be the most destructive attitude to take.

Each spouse should make the other aware of his anxieties when a change is planned. It is very helpful for each partner to admit what he needs from the other. The partner who is contemplating the change is often able to see this call for help as genuine and as a sign of real interest in continuing the relationship, not as an attempt to frustrate the change.

"I am afraid, and I will need your help if you want to change, because I'm fearful about it." This is a statement the partner can deal with. It indicates a wish to grow, too, and a wish to participate. To play the role of the panicked spouse is the best way to be rejected.

To state that the planned change is meant as a personal attack on you is a very destructive tactic. It is a way of saying that you don't believe it and feel the other is just angry. You must accept as the truth that a change is imminent, that the change is really what your spouse wants. To react in any other way is to say to the partner that you feel the change he is planning really doesn't mean anything to you. Nothing is more demeaning than not being taken seriously.

This may sound obvious and superficial, but it cannot be stressed too strongly. You should take your partner very seriously when he announces plans for a drastic change. Nothing hurts more than to be considered ridiculous by the person you want most to take you seriously. Try to imagine what is going on in the other's world. The months of thinking about the idea; the fear of admitting it; the wish to know for sure whether or not it will work; the self-doubts; the guilt; the hopes and the dreams all wrapped up into one possible idea. What will your partner feel if you don't take him seriously?

What is needed most at a time like this is someone who is willing to talk things over and to discuss the feelings about it fully and openly. Remember that one of your spouse's major stumbling blocks in making the decision has been the pain that he may cause you. It was a stumbling block because it made him feel guilty. To refuse to look is infuriating. There is no quicker way of removing another person's guilt than giving him grounds to be justifiably angry at you. If you adopt a very rigid attitude because you think this will keep things just as they are, rather than looking at them, you might well be removing all traces of your spouse's hesitation and allow him to act impulsively. So, to become resistant out of fear will work against you.

Don't say things you really don't mean and will be forced to back down on later. It isn't necessary to say something as compliant as, "If you want to leave your job and take up building bird houses in Vermont, it's fine with me. I'll follow you anywhere." That's like saying, "I'll have your baby." That's fine in a popular song, but not for real people. If you dread the possibility and you have no intention of leaving or any belief that you could ever tolerate life among bird houses, you might say something like, "If you want to start a new life, I think it's something we should talk about in detail, because it affects all of us." In time, you can bring up your feelings about Vermont, but it's a good idea to postpone hitting your husband or wife with a barrage of negative responses; none is likely to get through. The only sentiment that will be noticed is that you said "no," not what you felt.

If you deny entirely that you have any reservations when in fact you have many, you are being very unfair. In time, plans do get made and before you know it the date you thought would never arrive is here. You are supposed to be cheerful and whistling, all ready to go, but all you can do is fall apart. If you are afraid of saying "no" because you fear you will be abandoned, then your relationship is not an open one, one where you can express yourself honestly. It would be well to try and get your differences out in the open.

If you feel that by expressing your view you stand to lose a great deal, you are probably wrong. When two people begin to be honest with each other, they usually grow closer together even when that honesty is painful. In the face of an imminent change, being silent solves nothing.

You have as much right to what you want as your spouse, but you should be clear that you know what each of you truly wants. Is your wish to stay as you are really a wish to avoid confronting the world? Or is it a realistic expression of what you like and need? Do you want to stay in the same neighborhood because you really like it or only because you feel safe there? Is your home your real love or is it a refuge from the outside world where you don't have to think about anything new? In other words, do the routines and surroundings in your life merely serve your need for security or do they really fulfill you? Is your spouse sincere or is he just running?

These are questions that the two of you must sit down and work out to the satisfaction of you both. You must know what each feels about himself and what he feels about your feelings. Without this understanding, traces of doubt will interfere with your ability to give and to be supportive of each other during difficult times, even if you both agree on the surface. If you suspect that the other person really is only escaping, you should express your concern directly and ask him to convince you otherwise.

During these talks about change, it is crucially necessary to discuss what each of you feels the other's role is, and whether or not that agrees with the way each of you sees himself. It is surprising how often people who have been married for years do not know what the other person really thinks of himself. What a person is suspected of feeling is sometimes really nothing more than a projection of one partner's feelings onto the other.

A good example of this was a man I saw in therapy who assumed that his wife was violently opposed to his ideas without ever checking with her to see if indeed she felt that way. I eventually saw the two of them together and was able to show him that his wife was in favor of many of his ideas and was in fact very warm and supporting. It turned out that it was he who was afraid to take risks and needed someone to blame for his not feeling free to move ahead.

One of the greatest mistakes you can make at this time is to take a rigid stand categorically and to insist no matter what, that the old plans in the marriage, the ones agreed to long ago, must still be the ones to guide the two of you from this point on. Such a refusal to change is likely to force the changing partner out of the marriage.

If your spouse stays in the marriage in the face of rigid resistance (assuming that the change your spouse wished to make was a real one based upon new discoveries about himself), the situation for both will deteriorate. A spouse who is kept in his present situation by the other's refusal to budge finds it increasingly easy to blame all the faults of the marriage on the stand-patter. If you interfere with a change out of fear or through rigidity, you may live to regret your reaction. It will become the central point for arguments for years to come. Any time your spouse finds fault with you, this long harbored hostility, this seething resentment, will find its way into the conversation. You will be blamed for your spouse's unfulfillment over and over again. The failing in the present may be linked to your past resistances.

In time, even though it may not be openly discussed, your spouse will come to believe that all his failures are attributable to your refusal to allow him to start in a new direction. Something strange is present in such situations. If you are the sort of person who tends to act rigidly and not give in, your spouse probably knows it. Your rigidity is something that can be counted on. The best move in a situation like this is to allow your spouse to discover whether or not he can do what he wants. In time, in the absence of your anticipated objection, your spouse may begin to draw back and avoid the confrontation with himself. He may try to pressure you to object to his plans so he can blame something other than himself for not succeeding.

The rule is to give as much leeway as possible so there is time and room enough for the partner to find out to his own satisfaction his own limitations and abilities, or until he becomes afraid of failure and quits. At the point where your spouse knows more about his real chances, your discussions should begin again.

To allow yourself to become the unwitting target of blame for everything that happens in the household for the rest of your life is tedious and unnecessary.

The spouse of someone who plans to change and find new meaning in life has the opportunity to re-evaluate his own life and make it richer. Often, by being open and sharing the experience of change, a new level of mutuality, understanding, and trust can develop in a marriage. Sometimes the partner of the spouse who originally initiated the change becomes the one who benefits the most.

A spouse who wants to grow can be sometimes frightening and sometimes painful. But this much is clear: pretending that the threat is not there or that it will go away is unrealistic and only causes more hurt and anger. If the relationship between two people is basically good, an honest approach to change only adds strength to it and makes each partner more complete.

15

___

GETTING
READY TO GO

In the end, everyone who does leave a situation packs up his emotions and goes somewhere. You may not change anything except your attitude about life and living, but even that demands that you separate from some previous idea about yourself that you found restricting. Even if you pack up your bag and move around the world, but you do so without separating from your old ideas about yourself, you'll only take your problems on an expensive trip.

If you analyze your feelings about your situation and decide to change, it is likely that you have considered most of the important factors and problems you will have to face. But it is useful to talk. Much should be decided before you leave.

The new situation may be less taxing and less burdensome, but it may also require considerable financing and that is not always available. To begin a new life with unrealistic preparations is only to make it difficult at best; at worst, it guarantees to make the new venture unsuccessful and short-lived.

One way to begin preparing for a new situation is to start

in advance by cutting back your living expenses to what you think they would be in the new situation. It's best to do this as long as possible before you make the move so you will have the advantage of extra savings. If a spouse goes to work for some time before, this is also very helpful. If you are financially able to make the transition without too much difficulty, and most people are financially more able to make it than have the courage to admit it, then there is still the matter of having your routine affairs straightened out so that they demand minimum attention. You'll want to concentrate on your new enterprise.

Certain discussions must take place before you can make your move. Those with your spouse should be resolved and final plans in their modified form should contain some of the dreams of each of you. When most of the uncertainty about the plans has subsided, the children should be informed, and they should be allowed to express their wishes. To the extent possible, these should be included in the plans.

If a move is planned, the children should be allowed to visit their new surroundings beforehand as much as possible. Certainly the move should be discussed openly and as factually as possible, especially if it is out of the country. It is useful to have the children study any new customs and language beforehand. Initiating correspondence with children of their own age is very helpful. All along, the desires of the children should be taken into consideration, and they should be shown how they can be fulfilled in the new situation. Even if the parents only spend time discussing the terrain, the schools, or the availability of friends, talking makes the change easier. Finally, children should be told that they will be able to stay in touch with their old friends, that they will not be severed abruptly or permanently from them. Planning a return visit at the time when a break is being discussed makes the change seem less threatening.

Relatives who are in close contact should also be party to the discussions, but only after all the early doubts have just about been resolved. To bring relatives into the discussion earlier is usually tantamount to asking for their permission to do what you want to do. This rarely meets with the results you wish and only confuses the situation.

Much of the difficulty people experience when they make a change arises in part because they feel guilty about disappointing their parents. To move away from parents is always disappointing to them. To do so while one is planning a change in career from the one that made the parents happy is doubly so. Unless you are terribly sure that you know what you want to do or you feel that your relatives do not exert a clinging, guilt-producing influence on you, it is a good idea to wait before announcing your move. But don't wait until the very last minute, because that will only make people angry with you at a time when you least need it.

Once plans become settled in your mind, set a date when you plan to make the change. The date should be far enough away so that if you work hard it can realistically be met— but not so far away that you can easily put off thinking about it. Whenever dates are too far away, more than a year or so, people begin to lose interest in what they are planning and find it difficult to mobilize their energies toward it. Of course, if school or re-training is necessary, the waiting period may be longer. By way of consolation, the re-learning process itself offers intermediate goals, so you'll feel you are making progress toward what you want.

It is crucial that there be a sense of momentum toward whatever goal you do choose. The pressure to complete preparations because there is a deadline to meet will force you to move along, to leap over barriers that previously stumped you. There is a theory that the amount of work expands to fill the time available to do it in. You have wasted so much time up to this point that it seems silly to waste more. Why wait for an act of fate like a sudden physical collapse to convince you that you have limited time to do things? Your time is limited enough. Setting a date is the first order of business once your decision is made.

If you are working at a job, it will be difficult to keep others from knowing what you are planning, but remember that your plans cannot succeed unless you are able to make the transition smoothly. Because so many of your co-workers and associates will be jealous of you when they hear about your intentions, and because there is a tendency for people to gossip, you should keep your intentions to yourself as much as possible. The first person you do tell at work should be your employer and the time should be appropriate to allow sufficient notice. To speak up earlier is to invite being let go prematurely. If you are the boss, all plans should be kept absolutely unannounced until they are about to be put into action. To tell employees about such changes always makes them anxious and less productive. As a result, much hostility will be taken out on you through their inefficiency. Unless you are so guilty about abandoning everyone that you feel the need to allow them to punish you firsthand, there seems no need to tell them very early. This is especially true if you are planning to sell your company and the conditions of the sale depend upon its productivity. Revealing your plans too soon encourages people to rebel and to quit and to make your company worth less, leaving you with less capital to insure success in your new venture.

Some mothers who wish to take part-time jobs or begin a second career reveal their plans before they are really certain about what they want to do. If the announced plans are regarded as a threat, and the family responds in the way that makes them dear to everyone's hearts, everyone may suddenly find themselves unable to do anything on their own. Boiling water becomes a problem. Laundry gets piled high everywhere. Perfectly tidy people suddenly are unable to find the range or the bathroom hamper or to locate a jar of instant coffee. All these incompetencies are nothing more than an attempt to keep the poor woman where she is. If this reaction is anticipated, a period of preparation and training eliminates much of this undermining frustration.

If, in the end, you decide to keep things as they were after all, then telling other people will only have weakened your image and will have decreased your effectiveness and credibility with those around you. Again, it is a good idea to set a date and to tell people according to a plan when real developments will occur—and not just wishes.

The old saying, "Don't burn your bridges behind you" contains a great deal of truth, but it can work two ways. If a person acts too impulsively in making plans and putting them into action before he has really considered their impact on himself and on others, he may find himself trapped in a situation no better than the one he left. Indeed, because of all the sacrifices he has made, he may find himself considerably less well off. Plans should be initiated gradually, experimentally and with the understanding that only if each step works out will you go ahead. If the results are otherwise, you will reconsider and try another approach. To throw everything to the winds and run away calling back, "I've found myself at last" is usually doomed to failure.

It is just as difficult to succeed if no bridges are burned behind you. One reason why you have not been happy is that you have been spending so much time crossing back and forth between the bridges of your mind to visit this dreamland, imagining how nice it would be if you could do what you really want. Once you are certain that you are not happy where you are, and that this feeling is not a passing state of mind (even though it may not *always* be present), then the other steps are not more difficult; they are only more dramatic. Which is another reason why they should be taken gradually and according to plan.

Running away involves all the steps I have discussed in detail before: finding out what one wants, why one has not been able to do it before, why one feels guilty and so on. It involves making a commitment and setting a date.

It is only fair to point out that, in reality, there is no such thing as truly running away. "Running away" is the way we see someone else's change-making process when we feel trapped in an unpleasant way of life. If it were as simple as merely skipping off, a lot more people would have done it by now. The proper way to "run" is to go through the steps outlined in this book. It is actually a way of creating a second chance to do what you want most. Only the guilt of many years makes us see self-fulfillment as an escape.

Really now: is there any reason why you shouldn't do what you want? Why should you do something you don't want to do? Who but you knows that you are making a sacrifice by staying? Who can possibly appreciate fully why you feel so resentful? Obviously it is not simply a matter of giving in to one's desires, but managing the events and people in your life so you can have what you want. In all probability, the people around you, no matter how much they love you, will never be completely satisfied with the way you are or what you do. You are the only one who has to live your life.

The people and demands in our lives that get in the way of what we want can usually be placated with considerably less effort than we now exert.

We often displease people on purpose. Sometimes we just add fuel to the fire by talking about things we know will upset others. It is very easy to upset other people. We must realize that this is an extension of our angry feelings. There is very little purpose to making enemies and getting friends, and relatives, upset because we open our big mouths. If you want to placate most of the people close to you, just don't mention whatever you know will get them upset. And wait. That takes some doing. When you are ready to move, tell them.

What you cannot escape are your own feelings of being unfulfilled. You must put your guilt behind you, give up dreams you borrowed from others, dreams you never believed in. To the extent that you do not find yourself, to the extent that you do not look, to the extent that you do not try, you will be living a life that is not really yours. You will be at the demands of fate and the expectations of others for your happiness.

16

MAYBE YOU DON'T NEED RADICAL SURGERY

Only a fool living in a fool's paradise really believes he could always be happy. Any time I hear the protests, "My wife is the most wonderful person in the entire world" or "I think I have the best of all possible careers" or "I find that taking care of my family and house is the most rewarding thing I could ever possibly have done," I become very suspicious. Someone has got to have the world's most wonderful wife somewhere, I guess. But who can make that judgment? Someone has got to have the world's best job and someone, somewhere, is irrevocably convinced that being a housewife is *totally* rewarding. People who feel the need to protest so strongly are almost always fooling themselves. I know that will make some readers' hair stand on end, but it is true.

If everything is going great, there is little reason to advertise the fact. There is something wrong with every marriage if one looks long enough. I don't care who it is, who is married to whom else. The people who say that they have never had a fight in all their years of marriage just haven't talked about the issues that need airing. Another way of wording the same statement is, "My wife and I are only able to talk about things that we agree about," or "We have a profound problem in communication and are unable to tolerate any display of negative feelings," or "We are a rather rigid couple who finds it necessary to agree with each other and deny our hostility." Sorry to be so tough about that one, but I'm making a point that is often overlooked, though vital.

No one likes to admit it when things are bad. But from time to time things get pretty lousy in every marriage. If you are committed to maintaining a serene, beautiful appearing marriage—which means that you could conduct all your domestic discussions on local TV without embarrassment—then you also have a pretty up-tight little marriage. When anger does get beyond your ability to control it, and believe me some day it will, there will be an outpouring of feelings in great exaggeration. When the dam breaks, watch out!

Okay, I hope we are all believers now, able to admit that every marriage has its problems, every job its bitches, every household its drudgery and lack of fulfillment. We all have segments in our lives that are, frankly, a bit crappy to put up with, by anyone's standards, especially our own when we admit it. To the extent that this phenomenon is universal, and it is, it is impossible for any life situation to be perfect. But perfection is not what you are looking for. When discontent is major and more or less constant, the possibility for change and development of a new way of living is greatest. Since such discontent is present in all of us, it is usually possible to grow and to find new ways of expression and satisfaction in life. The reason why many marriages don't get better is that the partners are afraid to admit that anything is wrong.

If you are committed to the belief that everything is wonderful, so that you either don't lose face or don't have to admit that you made a bad decision, you will find it difficult to initiate any change. To alter the situation where you are trapped, you must admit being trapped. This is the bind where many people find themselves, and it seems unbreakable because of the commitment to being perfect. It sounds terribly childish and simple when looking at it from the outside, but it is quite painful, rigid and hopeless from the viewpoint of the parties involved.

Now is the time to ask: do you really have to make an overt and drastic alteration in order to be happy? Look around and ask yourself whether it is possible to have what you want in your life without the fundamental changes we have discussed so far. As I have repeatedly suggested before, much can be altered without upsetting your world.

The stifling sense of obligation that keeps people from enjoying life can be countered with, "Why not?" instead of, "I shouldn't." If you want to walk in the park with your shoes off and dangle them in a fountain as the kids do, go and do it. No one will even notice. Okay, maybe you can't spend all day there, but you can give up your lunch hour for it. It wouldn't kill you to miss lunch. Or is this too a big change for you?

What's wrong with taking some extra time in the day just for yourself? Why can't you just indulge in the pleasures you want and do this within the context of your present life? The point I want to make is that you can fulfill many of your wishes right now!

You cannot have everything you want, anyway. You cannot have the stars, but you can have most of what you want most. Start by ranking your wishes in the order of their importance, the order of what you want the most. Just making the statement, "I really want this more than anything else"—just admitting it and meaning it—is all it takes to begin to reach that goal. Much of what you have and do every day is not really fulfilling. Much of what you do takes time and money and you would do just as well without. Once you label the non-essentials, you will be able to spend more time doing what you care about. This means saying "No" to a lot of people. It means saying "Yes" to you, and aren't you more important? It also means that when you do give to others, it will be genuine and more complete.

The people you are going to say "No" to are often the people you have promised things to, not because you wanted to, but because you felt obligated. You can unobligate yourself to people just as easily. Just try saying, "For reasons that I can't go into now, I won't be able to do this anymore. I hope I haven't put you to too much trouble." Don't say why you are not going to do it anymore. That is only an invitation for an argument, and it sounds as if you are asking the other person to talk you out of your "foolishness" or get permission to say no. Remember you are going to be a little unsure of yourself and may be looking for ways to dilute your efforts so you can save face, just in case you fail even temporarily.

After you work for a while to squeeze obligations and non-essentials out of your life, you will find that you have a surprising amount of time and are now spending it with more things you like. You may be startled to discover how much happier you are. At this point, the wish to be somewhere else much of the time will become less strong. Your resentment and guilt may diminish and you'll feel surer about who you are.

We really don't do people a favor when we do things for them that we are unenthusiastic about or that rob us of the opportunity to do what we really want for ourselves. We resent it and the quality of how we fulfill such a favor, and the limited energy we are able to bring to it, reveals that. Our obligations take too much time and energy and leave us drained.

While it is true that you may not feel totally happy in your present situation even if you decrease your obligations, you will be less discontent than before and sometimes that is enough.

The biggest surprise to people when they have gone through much of the self-evaluation necessary to make a new life is that they *can* do it—and they can do it more easily than they originally thought. For example, the fears people have about losing a spouse often prove to be groundless. They discover that it may not be necessary to walk away from a marriage in order to change. That becomes a major discovery and is often a turning point for the marriage. If a wife believed that the husband was holding her back and keeping her from finding herself, she would feel resented, worthless, defeated, and each would believe that it was impossible to please or be pleased.

If you are resented because your spouse thinks you are holding him back from success as a person, then you must feel stupid or insecure. When your spouse discovers that it was his own insecurity (which he was afraid to test in the world) that kept him where he was for such a long time, substantial possibilities open up for growth and intimacy in your marriage.

The confrontation of one partner with himself makes life easier in the end for both, even if no drastic change results. At least the two partners become able to express their feelings more openly and to get closer together because they are fighting amid fewer defenses and pretenses. If the attempt fails, it still may be possible for the partner who failed to admit his own liabilities and to take them into consideration. The marriage can be upgraded to a new level of honesty. It is a chance for a fresh beginning.

While you can alter your existence dramatically without a switch of partner, job, location, or routine, it is always necessary to revise the way you look at the components of your life. The crucial issue is what is most important to you and how to go about getting it. Usually this question is avoided because it suggests dramatic upheaval. Whatever you need may indeed trigger a momentous upheaval of your life. Is that any reason not to look? The point is: whether you want to look or not, your feelings of discontent and hurt do exist. They flourish beneath the surface and gnaw away at you. Why not make yourself aware of them and at least know the name of the monster that is eating at you? You can't lose anything but your fears.

Even after a transformation you may not be completely happy with what you find. This is important to admit if it happens. The process of growth does not mean exchanging one situation for another, but, rather, moving from a limited and rigid way of living to an adaptable style characterized by continuous flexibility and growth. In such a new, fluid situation many decisions need to be made. Inevitably, not all of them will work out. Some will be wrong. There is no need to lament or to accept reverses as proof that the venture was folly in the first place. If you allow a setback to get you down, you only give strength to old patterns of denying mistakes and covering up inadequacies rather than dealing with them.

The new situation—just because it is more open and subject to further transition—may, in fact, seem to contain more problems than the old. That is not really true. Rather, you will just be aware of more since you now see more. In this frame of mind it is also simpler to solve the problems as they develop.

With the old way, unnecessary brakes keep you from reaching satisfaction in your life. The old way looks and feels bad. In the new situation, you can deal with problems more directly. If something indicates that a development is bad, you face it instead of pretending that nothing has happened. If it is correctable, you will now feel free to correct it. If another change is necessary, you will feel strong enough to undertake it. You really will.

Most people seem to have a vested interest in inertia, call it obligation, custom, the system, habit, fear. In the final analysis we are prisoners of our own fear of changing and the dread that we will be discovered for our previous mistakes and found out in our present hurts. To keep the mask up we expend our energies and live meager lives like puppets who move only when someone pulls the strings. We learn to hate a faceless puppeteer and take no consolation from our performance, yearning for the real world. We can reach that world—but only when we discover that we are our own puppeteers.